Essays on
Medieval Literature

BY

W. P. KER

London
MACMILLAN AND CO., Limited
NEW YORK : THE MACMILLAN COMPANY
1905

PREFACE

THESE Essays have all been printed before. The first of them served as an introduction to the first volume of Sir Henry Craik's *English Prose Selections* (Macmillan, 1893). The "Similes of Dante" appeared in the *Modern Quarterly* for March 1898. "Boccaccio" was read as a Taylorian lecture at Oxford, and published, in most honourable company, with other lectures of the same foundation—*Studies in European Literature*—at the Clarendon Press, 1900. "Chaucer" (part of a review of Mr. Skeat's edition) and the article on Mr. Macaulay's *Gower* are from the *Quarterly Review*, April 1895 and April 1903. The essay on Froissart (and on his English translator) was written at the request of Mr. W. E. Henley for the new edition of Lord Berners—*The Cronykle of Syr John Froissart*—in the Tudor Translations (Nutt, 1901-3). The last essay, in memory of Gaston Paris, is from the *Quarterly*

Review, July 1904. I have to offer my thanks to all concerned with those several publications for leave to reprint the essays. Nothing has been added, and little altered : here and there they have been trimmed, very slightly, in the phrasing, so as not to disagree with their present form. I am again indebted to my friend Mr. Paget Toynbee for his kindness in reading my proofs.

W. P. K.

London, *June* 9, 1905.

CONTENTS

THE EARLIER HISTORY OF ENGLISH PROSE

THE attraction of medieval literature comes perhaps more strongly from some other countries than from England. In France and Provence, in Germany and Iceland, there were literary adventurers more daring and achievements more distinguished. It was not in England that the most wonderful things were produced; there is nothing in old English that takes hold of the mind with that masterful and subduing power which still belongs to the lyrical stanzas of the troubadours and minnesingers, to Welsh romance, or to the epic prose of the Iceland histories.

The Norman Conquest degraded the English language from its literary rank, and brought in a new language for the politer literature. It did not destroy—in one sense it did not absolutely interrupt —English literature ; but it took away the English literary standard, and threw the country back into the condition of Italy before Dante — an anarchy

B

of dialects.   When a new literary language was
established in the time of Chaucer, the Middle Ages
were nearly over : and so it happened that for the
greatest of the medieval centuries, the twelfth and
thirteenth, the centuries of the Crusades, of the
Hohenstaufen Emperors, of St. Francis, St. Dominic,
and St. Louis, there is in English no great representative work in prose or rhyme.   There are better
things, it is true, than the staggering rhythms of
Layamon, or the wooden precision of Orm : the
Ancren Riwle is better.   But there is no one who
can be taken, as some of the writers in other countries
can—Crestien de Troies, for instance, or Walther
von der Vogelweide, or Villehardouin—there is no
one in England who can be taken for a representative
poet or orator, giving out what can be recognised
at once, and is recognised instinctively, as the best
possible literary work of its own day and its own
kind.   The beauty of medieval poetry and prose is
not to be found in England, or only in a faint
reflected way.   England did not possess the heart
of the mystery.   To spend much time with the
worthy clerks who promoted Christian and useful
knowledge in the thirteenth and fourteenth century
dialects of Lincoln or Yorkshire, Kent or Dorset,
is to acquire an invincible appetite for the glory of
other countries not quite so tame, for the pride of
life of the castles and gardens of Languedoc or

Swabia, for the winds of the forest of Broceliande. Not in the English tongue were the great stories told. Almost everything in the literature of the Middle Ages that is out of the common, that is in any sense magical or inspired, comes from beyond the English borders.

For all this want of distinction there is some compensation. The early English literature, if not representative of what is keenest and strongest, or most exalted, in the intellect of Europe in these times, is admirably fitted to convey to after generations both the common sense and the commonplaces of Western civilisation, from the ninth century onward. A study of English literature alone would give a very false and insufficient idea of the heights attained in the progress of European literature as a whole : for there were worlds of imagination and poetical art which were open to some of the other nations, and not at all or very imperfectly to the English. But English literature contains and preserves, in a better and completer form than elsewhere, the common ideas, the intellectual and educational ground-work of the Middle Ages ; and that is something. The average mind at any rate is well represented. Prose and its development can be observed very fully and satisfactorily from a very early date. One of the chief interests of the early literature is that it reflects the process by which the native Teutonic civilisation of the English became metamorphosed by the intrusion of alien ideas, either Latin or transmitted through Latin ; by the struggles of the English mind to overcome and assimilate the civilisation of the Roman Empire. Sometimes it is easy, sometimes not so easy, to distinguish the two kinds of thinking, native and foreign. The alliterative heroic poetry of the Anglo-Saxons is in-herited, not imported ; it is the product of centuries during which the German tribes were educating themselves, and making experiments in poetry (among other things) till they gradually formed the estab-lished epic type, which in essentials, in style and phrasing, and even in subject-matter, is common to Continental Germany and Scandinavia, in early times, along with England. It may be compared, even by temperate critics, to the Homeric poetry of Greece, and the comparison need not be misleading. The Anglo-Saxon prose, on the other hand, much of which is contemporaneous with the heroic poetry, is generally derivative and Latin in spirit, repeating and adapting ideas that are very far removed from simplicity. While on the one hand there are ana-logies with the Homeric age and the Homeric poems in Anglo-Saxon society and poetry, on the other hand there are many things in the work of the Anglo-Saxon writers which make one think of the way European ideas are now being taken up, without preparation, in the East—of the wholesale modern progress of Japan, and its un-Hellenic confusion. The spectacle is sometimes painful; it cannot be called dull. The same sort of thing, the conflict of the two realms of ideas, German and Latin, went on in all modern nations, beginning in the first encounter of the Northern tribes with the intellectual and spiritual powers of Rome. This conflict is really the whole matter of early modern history. In England its character is brought out more plainly than elsewhere, and, in spite of the Norman Conquest and other interfering circumstances, the process or progress is continuous. For which reason, if for nothing else, it is convenient to begin at the beginning in dealing with the history of English poetry or prose.

The work for which prose was needed first of all was mainly that of instruction; and of the early didactic prose a great part is translation or adaptation. From the time of Ulfilas to the time of Wycliffe and the time of Caxton, and since, there has been ceaseless activity of the workers who have had to quarry into, and break up, and make portable and useful, the great mass left by the older civilisations for the Goths and their successors to do their best with.

The early English literature is strong in translations. Translations were the books most necessary for people who wanted to know about things, and who knew that the most important questions had already been answered by the Latin authors, so that it was a waste of time for the English or other simple folk to try to find out things for themselves. The quarry of Latin learning was worked zealously, and the evidences left by that activity are more than respectable. The Anglo-Saxon Bible versions, and Alfred's library of text-books—Orosius, Boethius, Gregory, and the translation of Bede's history—are works which in point of style have attained the virtues of plain narration or exposition, and even something more ; and the matter of them is such as was not antiquated for many centuries after Alfred. It was long before the other nations were as well provided in their own languages with useful hand-books of instruction. Besides the translations, there were other didactic works in different departments. There is a considerable stock of sermons—some of them imaginative and strong in narrative, like the one on the Harrowing of Hell in the *Blickling Homilies*, and others, like the *Sermones Catholici* of Ælfric, more soft and gentle in their tone—more finished in their rhetoric. These may not appeal to every reader ; but the same might be said of the works of many later divines than Ælfric.

The old English educational literature—hand-books and homilies—had merits that were of lasting importance. The history of English prose cannot afford to ignore the books which, whatever may have been their shortcomings, established good habits of composition, made it fairly easy, for those who would, to put English words together into sentences, and gave more than one good pattern of sentence for students to copy. The rhetorical value of the didactic prose will be rated high by any one who values a sound convention or tradition of ordinary prose style for ordinary useful purposes. There are higher kinds of literature than the useful ; but it is something to have different kinds of useful prose at one's command, and this in the tenth century was singular and exceptional among the vernacular tongues of the North and West. In so far as the intellectual problem for the early English prose writers was the reproduction of Latin learning, they took the right way to solve it, and were more than fortunate in the machinery they invented and used to adapt and work up the old Latin materials.

The difficulty of the problem may easily be under-estimated. There were many things to hinder the adoption of a decent prose convention. There was, on the one hand, the danger of a close and slavish imitation of the foreign models. One is reminded by a clumsy participle absolute here and there that the temptation which was too much for Ulfilas also beset the Anglo-Saxons, who for the most part resisted successfully the temptations of foreign grammatical constructions, comparing well in this respect not only with the Grecisms of Ulfilas, but with the distracted participles of the Wycliffite Bible. The Latinism of the Anglo-Saxon prose is to be found mainly in the use of conditional clauses and a closer bracing of the parts of the sentence than comes naturally in primitive essays.

There was another danger besides that of helpless and slavish admiration of Latin syntax,—a danger perhaps greater, which was not so well evaded,—the tendency, namely, to get beyond the tones of prose altogether into something half poetical. Prose is more difficult than verse in some stages of literature, and where a good deal of prose was made to be read or recited, where the homilist was the rival of the poet or the story-teller, there is small wonder that often the sermons fell into a chanting tone, and took over from the poets their alliteration and other ornaments. This propensity to recitative of different sorts is common to the whole of medieval prose, and is worth considering later. Meantime there is matter for congratulation in the fact that so much of the Anglo-Saxon didactic literature should have escaped the two perils of concessions to Latin syntax on the one hand and to the popular taste for poetical decoration on the other.

The edifying and educational derivative prose is

what bulks largest, but it is not the only prose written in Anglo-Saxon times. There is another sort, and a higher, though the amount of it is woefully small.

If one is justified in discriminating what may be called the primitive or native element from the Latin or adventitious element in the old literature and the old civilisation, then one may put certain Anglo-Saxon prose works along with the remains of the heroic poetry, along with the lays of Finnesburh and Maldon, as showing what could be done without the aid of Southern learning in dealing with lively matters of experience, and the lives and adventures of kings and chieftains. If there were nothing to take account of except the translations and the sermons, there would still be room for satisfaction at the literary skill and promise shown in them; but it would be impossible to claim for the Anglo-Saxon prose more than the merit of being a vehicle for the common ideas of Christendom. But there is more than that; there are, besides the borrowed views and ideas, a set of notes taken at first hand from the living world, which have a different value from the homilies. The best of Ælfric's homilies are as good as the best of their kind anywhere. But that kind is the expository literature which sets forth ideas, not the author's own, for the benefit of listeners on a lower level than the author—his sheep, his pupils.

That is not the highest kind, and there is a higher to be found in the Chronicles, and in the narratives of the northern voyages brought in by King Alfred as an original contribution to his *Orosius*. The record of the Danish Wars, the voyages of Ohthere and Wulfstan, are literature of a more difficult kind than Ælfric's homilies, and literature in a sense that could never be applicable to any translation.

Of no old English prose can it be said that it is wholly free from Latin influence ; but in some of the varying styles employed in the Chronicles, and in the narratives of the voyages, one comes as near as one may in early English to natural prose—prose of the sort that might have been written by men who had nothing but natural English syntax, no Latin models of composition, to guide them. Prose such as one gets there is of the rarest near the beginnings of a literature. The last thing people think of is to put down in writing the sort of things they talk about, and in a talking style. These particular passages, and the navigators' stories especially, are good talk about interesting things, and, what is more, about new things. They are full of life, and strong ; there is nothing in them to suggest the school or the pulpit ; the people who composed them were, for the time, emancipated from the Latin authority, out of sight of land, the old land of traditional ideas and inherited learning. Here is to be seen what they

could do when left to themselves ; here is the true
beginning of independent explorations and discoveries
in literature. There is one sense in which it might
be no paradox to say that these passages, as compared
with Ælfric, for instance, are modern literature ;
being plain and clear accounts of real things, in which
there are no great corrections to be made on account
of any disturbing prejudices. The region of Ælfric's
homilies is distant and unfamiliar, but no one feels
any sense of strangeness in listening to Ohthere.
There is a clear northern light on his reindeer and
walruses, and the northern moors and lakes ; the air
is free from all the Idols of the Forum and the
Theatre. It was a happy inspiration that gave
Ohthere and Wulfstan their place in Hakluyt's
collection ; and indeed many of Hakluyt's men are
more old-fashioned in their style, and carry more
rhetorical top-hamper than Ohthere.

There were great opportunities for prose of this
sort—prose written in the tone of the speaking voice,
and describing the visible world and the things going
on in it. It is idle to inquire why there is so little
of such writing. One might have expected more,
perhaps ; for the literary talent of the Teutonic
nations, as far as one may judge from their poetry,
was all in the direction of clear and realistic narrative,
with no more superstitious accidents than were convenient in the lives of epic heroes, and no Celtic

vagueness or airiness, but a sense of solidity and matter of fact about the very witches and warlocks, as well as the hero and champion, their enemy. It may have been that in England, where the old epic style survived with wonderfully little modification to a late date, there was the less need felt for any epic prose. The poem on the Battle of Maldon (A.D. 991) has all the strong virtues of a dramatic prose history, and its poetic graces are consistent with prose sobriety. Perhaps if this close - knit and masterly style, this old simple epic tradition, had not maintained itself,—if the English war poetry had been dissolved, like its kindred in Norway and Iceland, into pure formalism and periphrasis,—then perhaps the history of the Battle of Maldon and the fall of Byrhtnoth might have survived as a prose history, with all its epic details and all its various individual personages. Byrhtnoth's adversary and conqueror, Olaf Trygg-vason, had his life written in that way, and the prose story of his last battle has more likeness to the methods of epic poetry than to such unimaginative history as the Anglo-Saxon Chronicles. But not much is to be gained by theorising in this direction, and the unrealised possibilities may be left to dispose of themselves. Only, in illustration of the prose genius latent in the old English poetry, one passage of the Chronicle may be remembered—the episode of Cyneheard and Cynewulf given under the date 755.

It is rude and harsh in its phrasing, but dramatic, with its dialogue admirably calculated and its sequence of events well managed : this passage is probably a prose rendering of some ballad. The situation is one that occurs again and again in heroic poetry and prose ; it is the story of kings fighting for their lives against their beleaguering enemies,—the story that never fails of an audience, whether the hero be named Cynewulf, Cyneheard, Byrhtnoth, or Roland. There is a great resemblance in general outline to the history of Maldon ; there is the same loyalty and self-devotion of the companions after their lord is killed. What is remarkable about this entry in the Chronicle, if it is really based on a poem, is that it has got rid of every vestige of poetical style which would have been discordant, and has kept only those poetical qualities, qualities of passion or sentiment, which are as well fitted for prose as for verse, or better.

There is little enough of such prose as this, but there is enough to take hold of. Together with such poetry as the poem of Maldon it forms the strongest part of the pre-Norman literature—" the stalk of carl-hemp " in it, compared with which the rhetorical excellences of Ælfric are light and unsubstantial. Contumely sometimes falls on the unreason, the vapidity, the garrulity of medieval discourses, and it is sometimes merited. At least it is difficult to refute the critic who says that he is bored by the conventional homilies and saints' lives. But for some things a strong defence may be made ; for all the old literature that " shows the thing right as it was," and gives adventures like those of Alfred and his men in the great match played against Hæsten, or natural history like that of the Finns and Esthonians. Medieval literature is not all monotonous recitative of traditional phrases ; some of it is fresh, strong, natural, and sane, and speaks in a tone of plain good sense.

This has sometimes been forgotten or ignored, both by those who have an affection for medieval literature, and by others. So many things in the Middle Ages are quaint and exaggerated and over-strained, and therefore interesting, that the sober reason and plain sense of those same times are in a fair way to be forgotten. There is more fascination at first in medieval romance than in medieval rationality ; the romance is beyond question, the rationality is sometimes doubtful. It is worth while to look out for places, like those already cited, where there is no trace of what is usually associated with the term medieval, no strained or feverish sentiment, no effusive and tautologous phrasing. And strong protest should be made against all attempts to over-lay, in translations or criticisms or otherwise, any of the colours of romance upon the simple fabric of plain stories. There is enough and to spare of

romance ; true histories are not so common in the
Middle Ages. They ought, whether in translations
or merely in the reader's impression of them as he
reads, to be purged of all unnecessary quaintness,
where such quaintness as they possess is due merely
to the old language, and not, as in much of medieval
literature, to a real element of fancifulness in the
author.

The two classes of early English prose, the derivative educational and the original narrative literature, are alike in this, that at their best they keep
clear of all unnatural intonations, and at less than
their best fall into chanting or recitative of one
kind or other. In the edifying literature there are,
as examples of the false style, the alliterative *Saints'*
Lives of Ælfric ; in the other kind of prose the
Chronicles themselves give a striking example of the
change of tone. They come to an end with the
lamentation of the Peterborough monk over the
miseries of the reign of Stephen. It is simple and
sincere, and in its way good literature, though it is
another way of writing history from that of the
voyage of Ohthere. Some of it may perhaps be
quoted again, well known as it is.

" Was never yet more wretchedness in the land,
nor ever did the heathen men worse than these men
did. For never anywhere did they spare either
church or churchyard, but took all the wealth that

was therein, and afterwards burned the church and
all together.   Nor did they forbear from bishop's
lands, or abbot's, or priest's, but plundered monks
and clerks, and every man another, wherever he
might.   If two men or three came riding to a
township, all fled before them and took them for
robbers.   The bishops and priests cursed them continually, but they took no heed of that, for they
were all accursed utterly, and forsworn, and cast
away.

"Wheresoever there was tillage, the earth would
bear no corn, for the land was wasted with such
deeds ; and they said openly that Christ slept and
His saints.   Such and more than we can say we endured nineteen years for our sins."

The pathetic and appealing tone of this marks it
at once as different in kind from the firmer and
more impersonal history of the times of Alfred and
his sons, and brings it into relation with all the
medieval literature in which the prevailing mood is
elegiac.   So widely diffused is this melancholy, that
one is inclined often to take it for the dominant and
almost universal character of the Middle Ages, as
expressed in books.   It belongs to devotional works
and to romances, to the Quest of the Holy Grail, to
the Romance of the Rose ; and even the strongest
and manliest writers—writers like Villehardouin and
Joinville—are often apt to lose their self-possession,

and let their voices break and tremble. Pathos was a strong solvent in the Middle Ages. It belongs especially, though not exclusively, to the later Middle Ages, to the romantic, not the epic age ; not to the matter of fact and stubborn people who fought on foot with swords and battle-axes, but to the showy knights of the Crusades, and the times when the world was full of ideals and fantasies.

In England there is one curious instance of the way in which pathos might be multiplied upon pathos. The *Ancren Riwle* (thirteenth century) is a practical book of instruction and advice addressed to a small household of nuns. It is not at all monotonous ; a good deal of it is kindly, humorous, and homely ; some of it is merely technical, dealing with the order of religious services ; some of it is moralising ; some of it is devotional. One part of it, the Wooing of the Soul, is beyond all praise for its pathetic grace and beauty. It was not left alone in its seriousness and its reserve. The theme was taken up again and treated with a dissolute ostentation of sentiment, with tears and outcries. The *Wooing of our Lord*, as compared with the passage in the *Ancren Riwle*, may stand as one indication of the sensibility and its accompanying rhetoric that corrupted late medieval literature in many ways.

There is so much good prose in Europe between the time of Alfred and the time of Elizabeth that

c

one may easily forget the enormous difficulties that stood in the way of it. Long after Alfred there still remained, as a disturbing force, the natural antipathy of the natural man to listen to any continuous story except in verse. The dismal multitude of versified encyclopedias, the rhyming text-books of science, history, and morality, are there to witness of the reluctance with which prose was accepted to do the ordinary prose drudgery. The half-poetical prose of Ælfric's *Lives of Saints* is to be explained as a concession to the sort of popular taste which, later, gave a hearing to prodigies like the *Cursor Mundi*, or, to take the last of the rhyming encyclopedias, written by a man who ought to have known better, the *Monarchy* of Sir David Lyndesay. The audience expected something finer than spoken language, and the taste that accepted the alliterative homilies may be compared with that which preserves the gaudy poetical patches in the Celtic traditional fairy stories, or that which requires from Welsh preachers that half of each sermon should be sung.

Besides the popular disrelish for plain prose, there were other distracting and degrading influences. The Latin models were not always as good as Boethius or Bede. Even Orosius, guiltless as he is of any brilliant extravagance, has his tirades of complaint, helping to spread the sentimental contagion ; and even Boethius, by providing pieces of verse for King

Alfred to turn into prose, encouraged an over-poetical manner of phrasing. The Latin Bible also, by its prose versions of poetical books, its parallelism of construction, its solemn rhythms, its profusion of metaphor, did much, unfortunately, to embolden the rhetoricians of the Church. The secular Latin literature, though it showed marvellous powers of recovering its decorum, yet was always prone to fall back into the wantonness that attacked it after the close of the Augustan age, when the poetical treasury was profaned and ransacked by magnificent prodigals like Apuleius. Even the later Greek Euphuism of the Greek romances found its way to England, through the Latin romance of Apollonius of Tyre, and ensnared an Anglo-Saxon man of letters, just as Heliodorus attracted the novelists of France, England, and Spain five hundred years later. The wonder is that any simplicity remained at all.

It is a long way from the tenth or thirteenth century to the sixteenth, yet in the age of Elizabeth the general conditions determining the growth of prose were not greatly different from those that obtained at the beginning. Latin literature was still the model, and still, in some cases, the too-absorbing model of prose. Still there remained the old temptation to excess of ornament, to poetical gaudiness; and though the Elizabethan rhetoric is different from Ælfric's, there is more than a chance likeness between the Anglo-Saxon Apollonius and the sugared descriptions of the Euphuists. And it was still possible for a strong-minded original man like Latimer to discard the conventions of bookish tradition and write the spoken language.

A great deal of prose was written between the *Ancren Riwle* and the *Repressour*, between the *Repressour* and the *Ecclesiastical Polity*, but the general conditions do not greatly alter. There was always Latin literature at the back of everything, with Boethius coming clear through the Middle Ages, to be translated by Queen Elizabeth in her turn, after Chaucer and King Alfred. There was always French literature to control and give direction to the English.

A volume of selections, beginning in the fourteenth century with Wycliffe, Chaucer, and the book called Mandeville, does not begin with any early improvisings of a style. The style of these writers is fully formed—a common pattern of style—common over all the countries of Europe. The reason for beginning here and not earlier is a reason not of style, but of vocabulary. The fourteenth century is not in prose what it is in poetry. There is no great revolution, like that which through the agency of Chaucer brought English poetry out of its corners and by-ways, and made it fit to be presented at the King's court. English prose, which had been decent and respectable hundreds of years before Chaucer, continued to be respectable after him. Prose was not affected in Chaucer's time by the revival of classical taste in Italy. The lessons of artistic construction which Chaucer learned from the poems of Boccaccio were not paralleled by any imitations in his prose of the classical elegances of the *Decameron*. The styles of Wycliffe and Mandeville are to be taken as specimens of that general level of composition which was the property of medieval Christendom, and one of the outward signs of the uniformity of its culture.

In the fourteenth century one need not be surprised to find that a good deal of the prose of all the countries of Europe is a little monotonous and jaded. For the general character of progress had been a levelling down of national distinctions, and a distribution over the whole field of the same commonplaces, so that one finds the same books current everywhere, the same stories : the popular learning in the vernacular tongues became almost as clear of any national or local character as the philosophy of the schools. Naturally, there was some loss of vigour in the process, and the later medieval writers are exhausting, sometimes, with their want of distinctive peculiarities, their contented rehearsals of old matter in a hackneyed phraseology. Prose literature taught and preached so much that it lost all spring and freshness; it suffered from an absorbing interest in the weaker brethren, and became too condescendingly simple. The childlike simplicity of medieval prose is sometimes a little hypocritical and fawning. Prose had been too long accustomed to talk down to its audiences.

In the fifteenth century there is something more than repetition of old forms. There are two argumentative books which are fresh and new—Bishop Pecock's *Repressour* and Sir John Fortescue on the *Governance of England*. It is a relief to come to these books which require thinking, after all the homilies and moral treatises which require merely to be listened to. The great prose achievement of the fifteenth century, and indeed of the whole time before the *Advancement of Learning*, is a book in many ways less original than those of Pecock and Fortescue. But Sir Thomas Malory's *Morte D'Arthur*, antique though its matter be, is singular in its qualities of style; and if the books of the Bishop and the Judge are remarkable for the modern good sense of their arguments, the *Morte D'Arthur* has its own place apart from them in a region of high imaginative prose.

Many things about the *Morte D'Arthur* are perplexing and even irritating. It is a free version of some of the finest stories ever made, and is based on versions of the multiform Arthurian romance, which

in some respects are beyond comparison the best.
Yet Malory has rejected some of the best things in
the " French book " which he followed. There is
nothing in Malory corresponding to the truth and
the dramatic sincerity of the first interview between
Lancelot and the Queen—the passage which Dante
could not forget. Malory never rises, as his original
here does, out of romance into drama. His refusal
to finish the story of Tristram is as hard to understand as to forgive, and as hard to forgive as the
Last Tournament. But when all is said that the
Devil's advocate can say, it all goes for nothing
compared with what remains in Malory untouched
and unblemished by any hint of dispraise.

Malory accomplished one of the hardest things in
literature. He had to rewrite in English some of
the finest of medieval French prose, full of romance,
and of the strangest harmonies between the spirit of
romance and the spirit of confessors, saints, and
pilgrims. What could be done in those days by
adapters and abridgers one knows well enough.
Caxton himself tried his hand on some others of the
Nine Worthies ; they did not fare as Arthur did.
To know what Malory really is, it is enough to turn
to Caxton's *Lyf of Charles the Grete* or *Recuyell of the
Histories of Troy.* Malory kept in English all the
beauty of the *Queste del St. Graal,* that strange confusion of Celtic myth with Christian dreams, the most

representative among all the books of the thirteenth century. The story suffers no wrong in the English version ; there as well as in the French may be heard the melancholy voices of the adventurers who follow the radiance of Heaven across the land of Morgan le Fay. The time in which Malory wrote was not favourable to pure imaginative literature—poetry was all but extinguished—yet Malory was able to revive, by some wonderful gift, the aspirations and the visionary ardour of the youth of Christendom—little in agreement, one might fancy, with the positive and selfish world described in the Paston letters. He did more than this also, as may be seen by a comparison of the French book, or books, with his own writing. The style of his original has the graces of early art ; the pathos, the simplicity of the early French prose at its best, and always that haunting elegiac tone or undertone which never fails in romance or homily to bring its sad suggestions of the vanity and transience of all things, of the passing away of pomp and splendour, of the falls of princes. In Malory, while this tone is kept, there is a more decided and more artistic command of rhythm than in the *Lancelot* or the *Tristan*. They are even throughout—one page very much like another in general character : Malory has splendid passages to which he rises, and from which he falls back into the even tenour of his discourse. In the less distinguished parts of his book, besides, there cannot fail to be noted a more careful choice of words and testing of sounds than in the uncalculating spontaneous eloquence of his original.

Malory has been compared to Herodotus, and in this the resemblance may be made out ; while, in both authors, the groundwork of their style is the natural, simple story-teller's loose fabric of easy-going clauses, in both there is a further process of rhetoric embroidering the plain stuff. Neither Herodotus nor Malory can be taken for the earliest sort of prose artist. Both of them are already some way from the beginning of their art, and though in both of them the primitive rhetoric may be found by analysis, they are not novices. Though they have preserved many of the beauties of the uncritical childhood of literature, they are both of them sophisticated ; it is their craft, or their good genius, that makes one overlook the critical and testing processes, the conscious rhetoric, without which they could not have written as they did. Malory's prose, and not Chaucer's, is the prose analogue of Chaucer's poetry,—summing up as it does some of the great attainments of the earlier Middle Ages, and presenting them in colours more brilliant, with a more conscious style, than they had possessed in their first rendering. The superiority of Chaucer's *Troilus* over the early version of the Norman *trouvère* is derived through Boccaccio from a school that had begun to be critical and reflective. Malory, in a similar way, rewrites his " French book " with an ear for new varieties of cadence, and makes the book his own, in virtue of this art of his. Much of the " French book " has the common fault of medieval literature— the want of personal character in the style ; like so many medieval books, it is thought of as belonging to a class rather than a personal author, as if it were one of many similar things turned out by a company with common trade methods. This is the case with some, not with the whole, of Malory's original ; it is not the case with Malory. He is an author and an artist, and his style is his own.

Malory, in much the same way as Chaucer, is one of the moderns. He is not antiquated ; he is old-fashioned, perhaps—a different thing, for so are Bacon and Jeremy Taylor old-fashioned, and Addison, and Fielding. The modern and intelligible and generally acceptable nature of Malory's book may serve to prove, if that were necessary, how very far from true or adequate is the belief that the beginning of the modern world was a revolt against the Middle Ages. The progress out of the Middle Ages had its revolutionary aspects, as when Duns Scotus was torn up in the New College quadrangle, and Florismarte of Hyrcania delivered to the secular arm in Don Quixote's backyard. But in literature, as a general rule, progress was made in a direct and continuous

line, by taking up what was old and carrying it on.
This at least was the method of Ariosto and Spenser,
of Shakespeare and Cervantes ; and their predecessors
in this were Chaucer and Malory. It is impossible
to draw any dividing line. There was no Protestant
schism in literature. One cannot separate the *Morte
D'Arthur* from the old romances on the one hand,
nor from the Elizabethans on the other. Malory
is succeeded by Lord Berners with his *Froissart* and
his *Huon of Bordeaux*, and Lord Berners is a link
with Thomas North, *Euphues*, and Sir Philip Sidney.
Innumerable classical and foreign influences went to
make the new world, but among them all the old
currents from the old well-springs kept on flowing.

If any apology is needed for concerning oneself
with the older English literature it must be this,
that the older literature has never been cut off by
any partition wall from the newer. Even the writers
least in sympathy with Goths and monks and
superstitions had at one time or other made excur-
sions into the enchanted ground. One finds evidence
enough of the favour shown to old books and old
styles of literature in days when there was no want
of brilliant new books. The Countess of Pembroke's
Arcadia kept its place in rooms to which the
Spectator found his way, and Dr. Johnson himself
(who accomplished the adventure of the *Loingtaines
Isles*) could be heartily interested in Amadis or

Palmerin. Perhaps the historians of literature have paid too little attention to the effect on the upper literary currents of this underflow of popular romance. At any rate this popular appreciation of old books will explain in part the success which attended the labours of Gray, Warton, and Percy, and go far to prove that the taste for medieval scholarship is not an imported fashion, and not anything to be ashamed of. Scholars like Gray, Warton, and Percy, like Scott and Ellis, had not to create the taste, for every one who read at all had passed through the stage of the *Seven Champions* and the *Seven Wise Masters* ; all they had to do was to clear up people's views of the importance of such like childish books, and display more and more fully the rich world to which they properly belonged, and from which they had come down. If any one objects now to the very early beginning of English literature, he may lay the blame on the nature of things ; for it is no capricious choice, no antiquarian perversity, that prevents this study from beginning comfortably with the Elizabethans.

There are grounds of expediency, indeed, making it best to set out, at first, with Chaucer. They are not reasons which affect the history of prose, or of English literature generally ; for the literature does not begin, any more than the constitution, in the reign of Edward III. It is convenient to begin where the language has come into something like its modern form, so as to get rid of the need for any large apparatus of glossary or notes. But the pedigree of English prose goes back beyond Wycliffe and Chaucer. It is not quite as long as that of the royal family of England ; it stops short of Noah and Woden and Cerdic ; but at any rate it goes back to Ælfred Æthelwulfing. That great king has been frequently threatened with ostracism, yet neither the political nor the literary history can do without him, and the literary like the political history of England is continuous.

In a book of specimens, which might be compared to a sculptured procession in bas-relief of orators and sages, one is forced to take a historical view, to consider the writers in their general relations to one another and to the whole of English history. Elsewhere and at other times they may be studied more minutely, each for his own individual sake. There are many dangers attendant on both kinds of criticism, and the critic who deals in generalities has not always the easiest time of it. Books of selections rightly made, from prose authors and poets, ought to clear away some of the difficulties. The characters of the several authors, and of the schools or fashions of thinking and phrasing to which they belong, are set out in such a way that they illustrate one another, and represent, page after page, the changing moods of the national life. These books do the historian's work for him better than he can do it himself. There are sceptics and nominalists who say that it is an abstract futility to talk of the "progress of poesy," or the history of English thought; that the real existences are not poesy, or thought, but poets and thinkers; that the historian, when he tries to be philosophical and bring in his cunning apparatus, his "evolution" and his "environment," is merely setting his petards to an open door. If those sceptics are wrong and to be confuted, they will be confuted, not by argument from the philosophical historian (to which they will not listen), but by the gradual and tentative creation, in the minds of readers, of a picture of literary succession,—such a picture as may be sketched out in an anthology, where one author is set off against his fellow, and where groups of authors compare themselves with other groups.

It is not perhaps of much importance to have a theory of literary history stated in fine terms, but it is a poor thing to lose appreciation of the different tracts and levels over which literature has passed—to be without the perspective of literature.

It is in the earlier periods especially that a truer perspective is wanted. The earlier stages have been left too much to themselves and to the specialists, with the natural result that the value of the later stages has been wrongly judged, most of all in the case of Tudor literature, bordering as it does immediately on the *terra incognita*. The revolutions and innovations, the glory and the rapture and the daring of the Elizabethans,—these things have been recognised ; not so fully their indebtedness to the poetry, the rhetoric, the literary skill of the Middle Ages. The Elizabethans are praised at the expense of older writers : they were not the first to whom beauty seemed beautiful ; the humanities were not brought into the island of Britain first of all in the Tudor times, nor are the humanities exclusively Greek or Italian. The Elizabethans lose nothing, but gain, on the contrary, by rendering their due to their ancestors—to the older practical writers who kept their senses unclouded by mists of allegory or superstition, and described the real world clearly— to the visionaries who went before Sidney or Spenser.

HISTORICAL NOTES ON THE SIMILES
OF DANTE

DANTE is the first modern poet to make a consistent
use, in narrative poetry, of the epic simile as derived
from Homer through Virgil and the Latin poets ;
and it is not too much to say that the use of this
device in all the modern tongues may be traced back
to Dante.   It was from him first of all that it came
into English poetry through Chaucer—both from
Chaucer's own reading of Dante, and also indirectly
through the influence of Dante on Boccaccio.   For
example, *Troilus*, ii. st. 139 :—

> But right as floures, thorugh the colde of night
> Yclosed stouping on hir stalkes lowe,
> Redressen hem agein the sonne bright,
> And spreden on hir kinde cours by rowe,
> Right so gan tho his eyen up to throwe
> This Troilus, etc.

This is exactly the simile in *Inf*. ii. 127 :—

> Quali i fioretti dal notturno gelo
>   Chinati e chiusi poi che 'l Sol gl' imbianca,
>   Si drizzan tutti aperti in loro stelo,
> Tal mi fec' io di mia virtute stanca.

Chaucer, however, does not take it from Dante : he had the *Filostrato* of Boccaccio before him, and there the passage is appropriated by Boccaccio almost word for word (iii. 13, ed. 1789 ; ii. 80, ed. 1831) :—

> Come fioretto dal notturno gelo
> Chinato e chiuso, poi che 'l sol l' imbianca,
> S' apre e si leva dritto sopra il stelo
> Cotal si fece alla novella franca
> Allora Troilo.

In the *Teseide* (ix. 28) Boccaccio varies the language :—

> Qual i fioretti rinchiusi ne' prati
> Per lo notturno freddo tutti quanti
> S' apron come dal sol son riscaldati
> E 'l prato fanno con più be' sembianti
> Rider fra l' erbe verdi mescolati
> Dimostrandosi belli a' riguardanti
> Cotal si fece vedendola Arcita.

It was in that way, sometimes by mere copying, sometimes by more original imitation, that this poetical device was made a commonplace in modern poetry ; and although, of course, later poets had access to the Latin authors whom Dante knew, and to Homer, whom he did not, still Dante can never be left out of account in reckoning up the obligations of later writers on this score. The authors chiefly studied by Spenser, for example—Chaucer in English, Ariosto and Tasso in Italian—are all in this respect the disciples of Dante.

The instance first cited has nothing peculiarly distinctive about it : it belongs to the common form, though it is not commonplace to the same extent as the epic similes of lions among deer, or wolves among sheep, which must have been of old standing long before Homer. A different kind of simile may be quoted from Chaucer to prove a different kind of poetical influence upon the disciples of Dante —the example of Dante's vivid imagination moving his scholar, not to borrow directly, but to think in a similar way :—

> Have ye nat seyn som tyme a pale face
> Among a prees of him that hath be lad
> Toward his deeth, wheras him gat no grace,
> And swich a colour in his face hath had
> Men mighte knowe his face that was bistad
> Amonges alle the faces in that route :
> So stant Custance, and loketh hir aboute.
>
> *Man of Law's Tale*, l. 547 *seq.*

There is nothing that exactly corresponds to this in Dante, but the character of Dante is stamped upon it ; it has the quality of Dante's imagination, as shown whenever he has to translate his emotional meaning into a pictorial image, and chooses to do so without going very far from his subject. This comparison in Chaucer of the anguish of Constance to the anguish of a man led to execution, whose face is dignified and made remarkable among the indistinct faces of the crowd, is not a simile from alien matter, like those in which an army is compared to cranes or to flies : it is a repetition of the same kind of situation, a case of another person under the same sort of distress. A large number of Dante's comparisons are of this sort : not analogies from something superficially different, but very close repetitions of the original, in which the poetic effect is produced by detaching and emphasising one particular aspect of the subject without alteration of its features. So in the simile of the gamesters at the beginning of *Purg.* vi., both the original and its illustration belong to the same order of things. The picture of Dante saving himself from the crowd of spirits thronging about him is of the same kind as that of the lucky gamester escaping from his importunate friends. At a distance, one might mistake the one scene for the other, and the imaginative value does not consist in any ingenious analogy, but in the vividness with which one aspect, one gesture, is singled out and brought before the mind :—

> Quando si parte il giuoco della zara,
>   Colui che perde si riman dolente,
>   Ripetendo le volte, e tristo impara :
> Con l' altro se ne va tutta la gente :
>   Qual va dinanzi, e qual di retro il prende,
>   E qual da lato gli si reca a mente.
> Ei non s' arresta, e questo e quello intende ;
>   A cui porge la man più non fa pressa ;
>   E così dalla calca si difende.

It is the great virtue of the Homeric simile—the simile of Homer, Virgil, Dante, and Milton—that although it has often been made stale and ridiculous, though it lends itself to any bad poet, and is fair game for every parodist, it is always able to recover itself. It is among the most commonplace of literary formulas, and still its freshness, its power of new life, is unimpaired. Not the *Rehearsal*, not even *The Tragedy of Tom Thumb the Great*, has spoilt the Homeric simile for the *Idylls of the King*, or for *Sohrab and Rustum*. In Dante's use of it, and in its effect upon his successors, is to be found one of the best proofs of the vitality of classical poetry in its influence upon the moderns. It is through the classical similes—capable of the most abject degradation, but also ready to spring up afresh in the mind of every new poet—among the oldest fashions in literature, yet inexhaustible—that the influence of Dante as the first scholarly poet, and the mediator between ancient and modern poetry, has been most clearly exerted. Dante's use of similes has been, directly and indirectly, a fructifying influence in modern poetry, akin to the influence of Homer ; keeping alive what is old in the tradition of poetry, but at the same time using the old forms in such a way that they act as stimulants to original imagination, and not as pedantic restrictions. Was he himself at all indebted to earlier vernacular authors, in translating the Homeric simile into modern poetical usage?

It is rather strange that there should have been so little imitation of the classical methods before Dante, except in the medieval Latin poetry, which made use of similes as a matter of course, as it made use, to the best of its power, of the classical vocabulary. In spite of the diffusion of Latin poetry, and a very general interest in grammar and rhetoric, there was for long a want of intercourse between the forms of classical and vernacular poetry. Ideas might be borrowed, the facts of history or mythology might be transferred from Latin into French or German verse, but the form of early poetry in the vulgar tongues is generally independent of classical influence. Similes, of course, there are, but similes were not invented by Homer ; they have a larger range than literature—they come by nature more easily than reading and writing. It is not the simile that is in question, but the Homeric expansion of the simile—that which makes it into a distinct piece of ornament, a picture in the margin of the narrative. Comparisons such as Homer might have used are common in the old French epic poetry, of which Dante probably knew more than he has expressly stated. But they are not used in the Homeric way. They are not made into pictorial passages ; they do not tend, like the Homeric similes,

and like many in Dante, to go beyond the exact
point of contact, into particulars that have nothing
to do with the likeness. Bolts fly like fine rain in
April,[1] warriors discomfit their enemies like a wolf
among sheep, or a falcon among small birds ; but
with that the comparison is ended : there are no
conventional set pieces, no " ac veluti," or " so have
I seen." One remarkable exception may be noted,
both on its own account and because of its correspondence to a Homeric simile on the one hand
and to Dante on the other. In the poem of *Garin
le Loherain*, a warrior goes through the ranks of his
opponents " like an otter through a fish pond, when
he makes the fishes hide in the water pipe " :—

> Ensement va com loutre par vivier
> Quant les poissons fait en la dois mucier.[2]

The same kind of terrified rush for shelter is rendered by Dante in his own way (*Inf*. ix. 76) :—

> Come le rane innanzi alla nimica
> Biscia per l' acqua si dileguan tutte,
> Fin che alla terra ciascuna s' abbica.

This simile is preceded by another one describing the
vehement onset :—

---

[1] In Ekkehard's Latin poem of *Waltharius Manufortis* a comparison
of this sort is treated with an amplification which, we may be sure, was
wanting in his German original : " Ac veluti Boreae sub tempore nix
glomerata Spargitur, haud alias saevas jecere sagittas " (*Waltharius*, 188).

[2] Ed. Paulin Paris, 1833, t. i. p. 264.

> E già venìa su per le torbid' onde
> Un fracasso d' un suon pien di spavento,
> Per cui tremavano ambedue le sponde ;
> Non altrimenti fatto che d' un vento
> Impetuoso per gli avversi ardori.

The Homeric simile is rather nearer to the particulars of the French instance than Dante's simile of the frogs ; in fact, the French simile might almost be taken as a translation of Homer into the terms of common life in the twelfth century. In Homer, instead of the fish-pond (*vivarium*), with its pipes, there is a harbour, and the invader is a dolphin, scattering the fish into the corners :—

As before a dolphin of the sea the other fishes are crowded into the nooks of a fair haven, stricken with fear, for verily he will devour them if he find them, so the Trojans huddled under the banks along by the stream of the grim water.—*Il.* xxi. 22.

Just before this there is another simile in the same matter, which is more like Dante's, and not so like the French :—

As under the stress of fire the locusts are wafted to the river ; and burning with indomitable flame it suddenly comes upon them and they shrink into the flood ; so before Achilles the stream of the deep-welling Xanthus was filled with the rout and noise of horses and of men.

The French simile has only one line of expansion, but even that is exceptional in the *chansons de geste* —an exception which proves the rule.   Both Homer

and Dante need two similes to express what they
mean, and the similes correspond to one another,
each to each : Homer's fire and Dante's storm,
Homer's dolphin and little fishes, Dante's snake and
frogs. They have the same way of looking at the
event, beginning with the tempestuous rush of the
conqueror, and ending with the disgrace of the
vanquished. The French poet sees clearly, and his
picture is true, but it is not his habit to spend
much on that kind of decoration. His one line
of explanation is already more than was generally
approved by those of his school.

In the modern poetry, which was of more importance to Dante than the French,—in the courtly lyrical
poetry, Provençal and Italian,—he probably found a
good deal that helped him, consciously or otherwise,
in his adaptation of classical methods. In this kind
of verse, unlike the French epic, there was some
definite attempt to secure the Latin art of poetry
for the benefit of the illustrious vulgar tongue.
There were, however, several things that told against
the classical simile in the courtly lyric. The simile
belongs to epic, not to lyric ; and though some of
the lyric poets in both the tongues show powers of
imagination akin to Dante's, they are of course
limited by their conventional subject. Their sentimental experiences afford no opportunity, or very
little, for pictures like those of the *Divine Comedy*.

Further, they were in command of an order of metaphor quite unlike the Homeric similes, and this kind of metaphor was almost as much a part of their conventional apparatus as the sentimental casuistry of their Art of Love. The distinction between the courtly lyric metaphor and the epic simile runs through the whole of modern poetry ; the two kinds seem to have nearly equal vitality, and they are seldom reconciled. The metaphors of the Provençal poets and the early Italians survive in Petrarch and all the Petrarchists, in all the courtly schools, in the "metaphysical" poets. Unlike the Homeric similes which spring up fresh from experience in Dante and Chaucer, the conceits 'of the courtly poets are handed down like heirlooms from one generation to another. As they were, so they continue ; the same in Cowley as in Petrarch, the same in Petrarch as in any poet of the first Italian century, or in any of the Provençals. They may be known at once : the similes of fire and ice, winds and floods—not those of the *Iliad*, but those of the despairing lyrist and the cruel fair one [1]—similes from certain parts of mythology, especially the *Metamorphoses*—Narcissus, Echo, Pyramus and the mulberry tree—similes from natural history, such as the moth (sometimes called a butterfly) and the

[1] Flames, sighs, and tears were of much more importance in Italy, especially after Petrarch, than in Provence.

candle — the Phœnix — the turtle — the basilisk.
These are among the oldest things in modern poetry
—at least they are found in the first courtly poets
of Provence ; but although they are so old, they come
again in every new school that has any pretensions
to be more refined in sentiment than its neighbours.
They distinguish Petrarch from Dante more than
anything else that is obviously demonstrable on the
surface of their poetry. Petrarch, with all his
modern ambitions, is quite content with these ancient
poetical jewels. His poetry was not of a kind that
perpetually demanded fresh illustrations from study
and experiences like those of Dante. The matter of
one of Petrarch's *Canzoni* (xiv.) is of the same kind
as in one by Inghilfredi Siciliano[1]—each verse devoted
to one of the favourite idols. Petrarch chooses the
Phœnix ; the Loadstone Rock ; the Catobleb, an
innocent creature with lethal eyes ; the fountain that
boils at night and freezes by day ; the fountain in
Epirus that kindles the quenched torch ; the two
fountains of the Fortunate Isles. Inghilfredi's selection is the Salamander, the Phœnix, the Tiger which
is pacified by a mirror, and the Panther.

Dante was, of course, a freeman of this guild, and
knew all their mystery as well as any of them. In
the *Divine Comedy*, however, he separates himself
almost wholly from their manner of thinking. Yet

[1] *Poeti del primo secolo*, i. 136 ; Nannucci, *Manuale*, i. p. 57.

there are traces of the old school even here ; it is true that he shows his divergence from it even when he makes use of its properties. The Phœnix comes into the *Comedy*, but not in the same character. Ovid supplies a number of comparisons—Pyramus, Echo, the spear of Achilles, and others—but not in the old context, though the simile of Glaucus has some affinity with the lyrical allusions, *Par.* i. 65. One of the very few metaphors used in the old way is that of the *emeralds*—

> Posto t' avem dinanzi agli smeraldi,
> *Purg.* xxxi. 116.

—where the allusion is evidently to the properties of the *smaragdus* in the old natural history : it is the most joyous of all precious stones.[1] This comparison may be reckoned along with those derived from *Physiologus* and similar authorities by the lyrical poets, some of which were classified and explained didactically by Fournival in the *Bestiaire d'Amour*, long before the fashion was revived in *Euphues*.

While the conventional established imagery was cherished and preserved by the Amourists in their lyrical verse, there were at the same time some of them who tried occasionally to get away from it. Among the Provençal poets there were some whose

---

[1] Nihil his jucundius, nihil utilius vident oculi . . . deinde obtutus fatigatos coloris reficiunt lenitate, nam visus quos alterius gemmae fulgor retuderit, smaragdi recreant (SOLINUS, 15, 24).

genius led them towards freedom, and some of the Italians, even under lyrical restrictions, anticipate the similes of the *Divine Comedy* in their vivid observation and their original record of experience,—for instance, Guido Cavalcanti, in the line—

> E bianca neve scender senza venti,

which is compared by Nannucci with *Inf.* xiv. 29—

> dilatate falde,
> Come di neve in alpe senza vento.

Guido's vivid line, it may be remarked, occurs in a sonnet of a very well-known type—that in which the beauty of the lady is described by comparison with all sorts of excellences in nature and art : one of the most favourite forms of praise in all the courtly schools. The lines of Guido and of Dante, though so much alike, have a quite different poetical function. In Guido the comparison is meant to enhance the beauty and grace of the lady ; in Dante it is to define and explain part of the adventure which he is narrating : the flakes of fire that he saw were like that.

One of the poems of Bernart de Ventadorn may be cited as showing both the direct original observation which is like Dante, and the ingenious learned analogy which is in the manner of Petrarch and the " metaphysical " schools. It begins—

Quan vei la laudeta mover
De joi las alas contral rai,
Que s'oblid'es laissa cazer
Per la doussor qu'al cor li vai,
Ailas, quals enveja m'en ve
De cui qu'eu veja jauzion !
Maravilhas ai car desse
Lo cors de desirier nom fon.

"When I see the lark moving her wings in joy against the light of the sun, and she forgets herself and lets herself sink, by reason of the sweet pleasure that goes to her heart; ah me, how great is the envy that comes upon me when I look on any joyous being! I marvel that my heart is not melted within me for longing."

The opening of this (which is not exactly a simile) must have been in Dante's mind when he wrote of the lark :—

Quale allodetta che in aere si spazia
Prima cantando, e poi tace contenta
Dell' ultima dolcezza che la sazia.
Par. xx. 73.

It is not quite the same thing, but it is observed in the same way as Bernart's, and rendered almost in the same tone. But when Bernart in the third stanza of this same poem complains that looking in the mirror of his lady's eyes he is in danger of the fate that befell Narcissus, the mood is changed alto-gether : Petrarch or Cowley would recognise their ancestor here, but this kind of imagination has little in common with Dante.

A poem of Folquet of Marseilles presents a similar contrast between the two kinds of imagery. The first stanza begins :—

Now that I am made aware thus late, like him that has lost everything, and swears he will play no more, I may well reckon it great good fortune, for now I know the guile that was practised by Love against me.[1]

The second stanza offers one of the many instances of the moth and the candle—a conventional elegant simile following on a plainer and less hackneyed comparison.

The Provençal poetry gives proof that the authors would have made more use of the simile if they had had more room for it : they were limited by their forms of sentiment, and could not illustrate the whole of experience from itself, but only the sentimental part : all their similes are applied either to the poet, or to the lady, or to the sentimental relation between them. While they are thus debarred from the wide region of narrative heroic poetry, with its succession of various adventures calling for illustration, they are nevertheless able to develop a kind of simile—a variation of the Homeric-Virgilian simile—which is taken up by Dante, and which makes one of the

[1] Sitot me sui a tart aperceubutz.

BARTSCH, *Chrest. Prov.* 123.

characteristic differences between his poetry and the
common form of epic. The Provençal poets did the
best they could to illustrate their own sentimental
dispositions and circumstances by means of similes.
The kind of illustration that they found most convenient was that derived from the *Saints' Lives of
Cupid*, the history of true lovers in the past, Paris
and Helen, Tristan and Ysolt, or from the traditional
natural history with its moral signification. Besides
this, however, they occasionally tried to vary their
poetry with other and more original comparisons,
modelled upon those of Latin heroic poetry. They
had to bring the Homeric simile into the service of
lyric poetry, to illustrate the fortunes and the moods
of distressed lovers. Here Dante followed them,
while he followed the freer narrative poets as well.
Like the epic poets he uses similes for any adventure
that may fall to be described : like the Provençal
lyric poets he uses the simile for the changes in his
mind. His poem is not purely epic ; it is descended
in one line from the *sirventes*, the lyrical satire of
the Provençals, and in so far as the mind of the poet
is the subject of the poem, so far is the Provençal
lyrical simile applicable. Hence the great number
of similes that follow the pattern of the first in
the book.

E come quei che con lena affannata, etc.

The instance from Folquet quoted already is one

of this sort, and there are others of different kinds. Four of the poems of the Monk of Montaudon begin " Aissi com cel," or " aissi com om," which answers precisely to the Italian " come quei." [1]

In all these cases the subject is the poet himself. " As one who has lived long in peace on his own freehold without a lord, and afterwards is by an evil lord put under constraint."

" As one who is losing a bad case at law, and dare not hear the judgment, and willingly would leave it all to two friends to bring about a good agreement, so would I fain do in the pleas of love."

" As one who is in an ill lordship, and gets no grace, but is taxed and tolled, and would gladly change his estate, so gladly would I escape from her dominion who has taken my life."

" Even as one who is persecuted by his lord, and begs for mercy, but his lord will have no mercy, and holds him fast till he has paid his ransom."

Other instances of a similar kind might be found without much difficulty ; *e.g.*, Pons de Capdoill :—

> Aissi m' es pres con sellui que cerquan
> Vai bon seignor, etc.

---

[1] Aissi com cel qu' a estat ses seignor (p. 10).
Aissi com cel qu' a plait mal e sobrier (p. 14).
Aissi com cel qu' es en mal seignoratge (p. 20).
Aissi com om que seigner ochaizona (p. 28).
Ed. Philippson, 1873.

These all resemble Dante's similes about himself, and differ from the common run of conceits in their evident intention of bringing out the literal meaning of what they illustrate. They are not extravagant or far-fetched; as ornament they have little to take the fancy; they are quite unlike the ornamental work composed of the Phœnix and the Basilisk. The poet keeps close to his subject, and the reality is too strong to be dissipated in imagery.

The similes of the *Divine Comedy* might be classified according to their greater or less variation from the ordinary epic type. Some keep very closely to the old form, like that of the snake and frogs already noticed, which illustrates part of the action of the poem in a way that has every right to the name Homeric. The first step of divergence from this type is due to the difference between Dante's poem and all other epics. The business of his poem is not the common matter of feasting and fighting and parliaments: he requires fewer similes in order to give variety to familiar scenes: his object is to give clearness of detail to a personal narrative: hence the great number of similes which give the right, accurate description of a thing, and not a comparison with something else: *e.g.* the famous passage about the pitch in Malebolge is Homeric in its digression, its description of what goes on in the arsenal at Venice, but the central part of the simile is unlike

E

Homer, for it is merely meant to tell you what the pitch exactly was, not what it poetically resembled.

When Homer compares the wound on Menelaus's thigh to the purple stain on ivory,[1] the work of a Mæonian or a Carian woman, and then goes on to think of the uses to which the ivory may be put as an ornament for harness, the digression may appear to have the same sort of value as Dante's description of the dockyard : neither has anything to do with the story. But the original motive is quite different : Homer is moving away from the subject—he does not wish to make you see the blood more clearly, but to translate it poetically into something different ; whereas for Dante the meaning of the comparison is in the matter of fact which it contains : Venetian pitch is not an illustration, but, as near as may be, an equivalent for the thing which he wishes to bring as exactly as possible before the mind.

To this class belong the great number of local comparisons in the *Inferno* : there are hardly any in the *Purgatorio*, and none in the *Paradiso* :[2] because the country in the *Inferno* is more varied and difficult, and requires some notes from more familiar scenery in order to explain as clearly as possible what it is like.

---

[1] *Il.* iv. 141 *sqq.*

[2] None, at any rate, of the same kind as those most usual in the *Inferno*. The Chiana is introduced in the *Paradiso* (xiii. 23), but merely for the slowness of its stream, as an example of slowness, and an illustration of what is *not* in the poet's vision.

Much greater deviation from Homer is occasioned
by the need for illustrations of the changes in the
mind of the narrator, and it is here that Dante may
possibly have derived some hints from the practice
of the lyrical poets in the vulgar tongue. They also
provided him with one very considerable class of
illustrations, for any kind of subject, by their fondness for references to Ovid and other poets ; not
excluding the contemporary romances. Bertran de
Born, in one poem, refers both to Gawain and to
the story of William of Orange ; and a less famous
poet, Richart de Berbezill, makes a beginning, in
one case, by comparing himself to Percival, who was
silent when he should have spoken, and failed to ask
the meaning of the Lance and of the Grail.[1] The
literary similes of Dante, as well as those arising
from his own states and changes of mind, may be
put down pretty certainly to the credit of his Provençal studies.

[1] " Atressi com Persavaus."
Parnasse Occitanien, p. 276.

BOCCACCIO

To many readers it has appeared as if the friendship of Petrarch and Boccaccio made the first comfortable resting-place in the history of literature, on this side of the Dark Ages. On the other side, farther back, there are no doubt many marvellous and admirable things, the enchantments and sublimities of " Gothic " art ; but there is little rest there for those who are accustomed to the manners of the earlier literature. There are interesting things, there are beautiful things in the literature of the Middle Ages ; poems and stories that have character and worth of their own, and cannot be displaced or annulled by anything the Renaissance or the march of intellect may have produced in later times. But there is one defect in the Middle Ages : they are not comfortable. There is no leisurely rational conversation. Many civilised and educated persons feel on being asked to consider medieval literature, to pay attention to the poets of Provence or to the Minnesingers, the same sort of reluctance, the same need for courage, that Dr. Johnson may have felt in setting out for the Isle of Skye. Even to speak of Dante is not always safe with the less adventurous sort of pilgrims ; it is like recommending a good mountain to a traveller who is anxious about his inn. Boccaccio and Petrarch come much nearer to their readers and take them into their confidence ; they make friends for themselves as only modern authors can, or authors who belong to an age like that of Cicero or Horace, in which there is conversation and correspondence and a vivid interest in the problems of literature. The reader who is acquainted with the Epistles of Horace may be pleased to think that in the society of Petrarch and Boccaccio he has escaped from the Goths—he has arrived at the familiar world where there is an intelligent exchange of literary opinions. Petrarch and Boccaccio have made this sort of reputation for themselves. It may be fallacious in some respects ; the explorer who goes to the Letters of Petrarch will do well for his happiness if he forgets to compare them with the letters of Cicero or of Swift. But the impression is not altogether wrong ; Petrarch and Boccaccio, in their conversation, are more like the age of Lewis XIV. or of Queen Anne than any authors in the thousand years before their day.

Those two Italian poets have the advantage—an unfair advantage possibly—over older writers that they do not depend for their fame altogether on the present value of their writings. They have imposed their story on the world, their hopes, interests, ambitions, and good intentions. Like Erasmus and Rousseau, they are known to the world, and esteemed by the world, without very much direct and immediate knowledge of their writings. There is a traditional legend of their quest for the sources of learning, and for perfection in literature. Also there is, apart from their individual works, the historical and dramatic interest of their contrasted characters. The merest fragments of knowledge about the two Italian poets, the traditional story of Laura, the garden of the *Decameron*, may set one's fancy to work on a story of two scholarly friends who were brought together by their genius and their ambition, and eternally kept from understanding one another through a difference of humour in their natures. It is a situation such as is familiar in comedy. There are two men who are friends and associates : one of them, Petrarch, is an enthusiast, full of sensibility, full of anxiety, troubled about his soul, troubled about his fame, vexed with distracting interests, and with a mind never safe from the keenness of its own thoughts—an unhappy man from the hour of his birth. The other, Boccaccio, is equable and sanguine, takes the world lightly, is not inclined to make grievances for himself nor to remember

them ; at the same time a hard worker, yet not dis-
tressing himself about his work ; possessed of those
happy virtues of which Bacon speaks, for which it is
difficult to find an appropriate name. " The Spanish
name *disemboltura* partly expresseth them, when
there be not stonds nor restiveness in a man's
nature, but that the wheels of his mind keep way
with the wheels of his fortune." He acknowledged
himself the pupil and follower of Petrarch. He was
more even-tempered and happier than his master, but
far inferior to him in scholarship and insight. Boccaccio recognised this, and did his best to profit by
Petrarch's example and instruction. His Latin prose
and verse must have seemed doubtful to Petrarch ;
one can only guess what pain the better scholar
suffered and dissembled in reading the essays of
Boccaccio. That is part of the comedy ; the best
part of it is that both the personages retain their
separate characters unspoilt and uncompromised in
what might seem to have been a remarkably hazardous exchange of sentiments and opinions. To the end
the relations are maintained between them : Petrarch
is always the master, and never entirely at liberty,
never contented ; Boccaccio always acknowledges
that he is a pupil, and is always unconstrained.

Two of the differences between them, which might
seem promising occasions for a downright quarrel, but
really turn out quite otherwise, are to be found in

Boccaccio's expostulation with Petrarch on his residence at Milan with the Visconti, which he regarded very naturally as a surrender to a tyranny, and in his letter accompanying a copy of Dante's poem. To explain to your friend and master that he is selling his soul, to remind Petrarch of the genius of Dante, these ventures might be thought to be dangerous; it is difficult to see any good answer to a friend who tells you ever so considerately that you are turning against your principles.

As to the shamefulness of Petrarch's yielding to the attractions of Milan, he had no good answer ready; what defence he tried to make must be reckoned among the least admirable things in his history. He had not to meet Boccaccio only, but a host of other critics. Boccaccio (in 1353) had put the case as gently as he could, in the form of an allegory, but his touch was not light. Italy, neglected and betrayed, is represented as Amaryllis, and the Archbishop of Milan, Petrarch's friend, as Aegon priest of Pan, who has abandoned his rural worship and made himself into a captain of thieves. It is with this renegade that Silvanus (Petrarch's own name for himself in the eclogue to his brother) has allowed himself to betray the Muses and the Peneian Daphne (that is, Laura), and what is he doing there? It is not indeed to be thought that, along with Aegon, he is glad to hear of murder and rapine, the shame and desolation of his native land ; yet what is the friend of solitude, of virtuous freedom and of poverty, what is Silvanus doing in that tyrannical house ?

The allegory does not do much to soften the accusation. What Petrarch said to Boccaccio in answer is not known, but the lines of his defence are found in letters to other correspondents. They are not good. The power of the great to command obedience, the vanity of human wishes,—these are made his excuse. There may have been insincerity on both sides ; it is probable that Boccaccio did not feel the shame of submission as vehemently as he was able to express it. Yet, however it is taken, the situation is characteristic of both parties, and so is the result. Boccaccio is on the side of the obvious and superficial truth ; the man who praised solitude, independence, and poverty, and who has wished, in immortal verse, that he could awaken Italy from her lethargy of servitude, is not the man to accept any patronage from the Visconti. Petrarch, on the other hand, finds himself driven from the plain ground into sophistical apologies. He has to make himself believe what he wishes, and in the fluctuations of his life he supports himself on the commonplaces of the moralists. There is no quarrel, but the men are different.

The difference comes out much more distinctly,

and we may say the danger of a breach between them is very much greater, in the case of the letter about Dante. A matter of personal conduct was never very serious to Boccaccio, where it did not touch his own interests, and not always then ; but on some questions of taste he would venture a good deal. It is unlikely that he would have stood a long examination on the rack ; but one of the last things he would have renounced was his admiration for the *Divine Comedy*. The words put in his mouth by Landor, in the imaginary conversation with Petrarch about Dante (*Pentameron*, First Day), are perfect as a summary of his ways of thinking. Petrarch says to him : "You are the only author who would not rather demolish another's work than his own, especially if he thought it better—a thought which seldom goes beyond suspicion." And Boccaccio answers, in terms that really represent his character : " I am not jealous of any one ; I think admiration pleasanter."

He sent a copy of Dante's poem to Petrarch in 1359, with some Latin verses, the purport of them being to inquire why Petrarch was unjust to Dante. He does not say as much as this explicitly, but the meaning is plain enough. It is a common incident. Imagine a zealous admirer of Mr. Browning's poetry sending a copy of *The Ring and the Book* to a severe and critical friend. " You must read this : ' Because, you spend your life in praising, to praise you search the wide world over ' ; how have you been able to go on for years without saying a word about this glorious poem ? " And the recipient of these benefits, when he has time to spare, goes calmly and writes a letter more or less like Petrarch's answer to Boccaccio, and is the cause of grief and surprise in the mind of the enthusiast. " You are mistaken in supposing that I ever undervalued your poet ; on the contrary, I have always consistently pitied him, on account of the wrong done to him by his foolish admirers. It is true that I never read much of him, for at the usual age for such things I was on other lines, and had to be careful about desultory reading. Now, of course, I shall take your advice and look into him again, I hope with good results. I need not say"— and so forth.

It is much in that way that Petrarch thanks Boccaccio for his present ; and still they were friends. Some historians have found that Petrarch is cleared by his letter from the suspicion of envy, but it is not easy to find any very sincere good will to Dante or his poem. It was impossible for Petrarch to share Boccaccio's honest, unreserved delight ; he had prejudices and preoccupations ; he was obliged to criticise. Boccaccio has no hesitations, doubts, or scruples ; his fortunate disposition makes him a thorough-going partisan of what he feels to be good. He does not criticise : he thinks admiration pleasanter.

These two authors, so unlike in most things, were brought together by friendship and common interests, and have their place together in history ; they are among the first of the moderns in every account of the revival of learning, and they are reverenced as among the first explorers and discoverers by most writers who have to describe the emancipation of humanity from the superstitions of the Middle Ages.

It may be suggested that possibly the historians of the Renaissance have been a little too much inclined to interpret the fourteenth century by their knowledge of the sixteenth, to read Petrarch by the light of Montaigne. Montaigne is what it all ends in, no doubt,—in Montaigne, or in Shakespeare. There at last, in the prose author and in the poet, is the explanation and solution of those difficulties in which the life of Petrarch is involved ; and Petrarch takes the first stages in a progress that is to lead from superstition (that is to say, the traditional and conventional moralities of the Dark Ages) to the free and unembarrassed study of human nature. It is impossible to understand Petrarch without the sixteenth century. But Petrarch did not travel the whole course ; though all his life is an effort to get freedom, he never fully escapes from the ancient ways. It is a mistake in history to represent him as conscious of the full meaning and import of his reforms in learning and in poetry. Many things he saw clearly, but he was never free from the medieval hindrances, and he feels them more than those who have no glimmering of any other world outside their medieval cave. In Boccaccio there are like contradictions, but here the difference of temper in the two men comes and helps the more sanguine of the two. Boccaccio does not feel the contradictions in the same degree as Petrarch, and does not fret about them.

Where the weight of medieval convention is most obvious in the writings of Petrarch and Boccaccio, is perhaps in their theories of poetry. The work of Petrarch in Italian verse is often described, and justly, as if it were a victory of form and poetic style, of pure art not distracted from its own proper aims. But there is no hint of this sort of view in Petrarch's own descriptions of the poetical office. On this subject he speaks out quite distinctly ; he has no hesitation at all, nothing but unqualified and uncompromising adherence to the doctrine that all poetry is allegory (*Fam*. x. 41, to his brother)—the doctrine that filled the Middle Ages with their most tedious fictions and conventionalities, the doctrine that provokes more scorn and invective than any other from the leaders of the new schools, equally in religion and in learning. Tindale the reformer speaks of it in terms not very different from those of Rabelais.

Boccaccio holds this medieval doctrine also, but he holds it in his own characteristic way. He is fond of it, and especially fond of a quotation from St. Gregory the Great, the chief authority on the allegoric method. St. Gregory, in the preface to his *Moralia*, explains that the Holy Scripture is not for one order of mind only—that it may be read by simple people in the obvious sense as well as by great clerks in the allegorical. Boccaccio adopts St. Gregory's illustration, and speaks of poetry, and incidentally of his own Commentary on Dante, as giving both the easy and the difficult meaning. " It is like a river in which there are both easy fords and deep pools, in which both the lamb may wade and the elephant may swim "—*un fiume piano e profondo, nel quale l' agnello puote andare, e il leofante notare.*

But while Petrarch holds to this doctrine painfully, and expounds the *Aeneid* as an allegory of man's soul, and his own eclogue to his brother Gerard the Carthusian, minutely, point for point, as an allegory of his studies, it never is allowed to trouble Boccaccio. His apology for poetry in the *De Genealogia Deorum*, though it keeps to this medieval commonplace about the allegorical mystery of poetry, is full of life and spirit. One of the best pieces of satire since Lucian discussed the professional philosophers is Boccaccio's account of the way the schoolmen on the one hand and the friars on the other go depreciating poetry and crying up their own wares instead. Who are the men who revile the Muses ? There is a race, he says,

who think themselves philosophers, or at any rate
would be glad to be thought so, who say that poetry
is all very well for children in their grammar schools ;
they are men grave in language and ponderous in
their manners, who trade in words that they have
gathered from glances at books—words that do not
touch reality ; who trouble learned men with their
problems, and when they are answered, shake their
heads and smile at the rest of the company, as if it
were nothing but respect for the years of their
instructor that prevented them from crushing him ;
then they will go and make use of what they have
heard and give it out as their own, if they can get
any one to listen to them, musing and sighing as if
they were in deep contemplation, or as if they were
drawing true oracles direct from their most divine
and mysterious sources. The allegorical theory of
poetry does not look so formidable when Boccaccio is
explaining it. His defence of poetry is much the same
as Sir Philip Sidney's, and seems to have been called
out by the same kind of puritan depreciation as Sidney
had to refute. Once in his life, it is true, Boccaccio
was seriously frightened and made to doubt whether
a lover of poetry could be saved,—through a warning
from the deathbed of a certain religious man, who had
a vision of Petrarch and Boccaccio, and sent them
notice of their probable fate if they persisted in carnal
learning and poetry. Petrarch had to encourage him,

and advised him not to be seriously troubled.   In this distress the allegorical theory may have been a comfort to Boccaccio.   But practically it has very little effect on his work ; and many poets of a much later day, like Tasso, allow it a much more important place in their poetical designs.

It is hardly possible to make too much of the influence of Petrarch and Boccaccio on the literature of Europe.   Both of them depended upon the older medieval poets for much of their own writing : Petrarch on the earlier schools of courtly verse, Provençal and Italian ; Boccaccio on French romances, on the *Divine Comedy*, and on the popular narrative poetry of his own country ; but while both were largely in debt, both made such use of what they borrowed that they gave their own character to the medieval forms ; and so everywhere in later ages the form of courtly lyric is mainly Petrarchian, not in Italy only, but in all the Latin nations and in England, with Ronsard, with Camoens, with the Elizabethans ; while the most successful forms of narrative poetry are those which Boiardo, Ariosto, and Tasso derived from the work of Boccaccio, and handed on to Spenser.   Petrarch and Boccaccio determined the course of the principal streams of poetry in all the languages of Europe for more than two centuries after their lifetime, and, in some important respects, even to the present day.

As a successful inventor of definite literary forms, as the founder of literary schools, Boccaccio may claim respect for all his works, and not for his one great book, the *Decameron*, only. Even if the *Decameron* had never been written, there would still remain a great variety of things in prose and verse, each with some original value of its own, and all, even the least successful of them, productive and stimulating in the schools of poetry.

The *Decameron* has perhaps had less influence in this way, as a pattern of literary design and execution, than some of the other works of Boccaccio—the *Teseide* for instance. The *Decameron* has provided matter for a great number of authors—Dryden in the *Fables*, Keats's *Isabella*, and later still ; but the form and the expression of the *Decameron*, which are its great excellence, have not been copied to the same extent, or at any rate in the same obvious and acknowledged manner. It doubtless made the first great and decisive change from the naïve and unstudied fashions of medieval composition to the elaborate harmonies of prose ; and again, wherever in later comedy the vernacular of vulgar speech is liberally used, there may be found something to recall the rich idioms of Bruno and Buffalmacco, and the other Florentine ruffians of the *Decameron*. Yet the *Decameron* is not followed in the same way as some of the less famous works of Boccaccio. The *Filocolo*, the *Filostrato*, the

Teseide, the *Fiammetta*, the *Ameto*, are each a new kind of fiction, showing later writers some of the promising ways in which their ideas might be arranged and developed.

The *Filocolo* and the *Fiammetta*—works which have their faults—are among the most ingenious and dexterous examples of literary tact. They are types of prose romance which were wanted in modern literature. Boccaccio discovered these new and promising varieties of story, apparently without any trouble or labour. The *Fiammetta* is the first of the prose romances in which the heroine is made the narrator, and in which vicissitudes of sentiment are the matter of the story. He had certain models to work upon ; chiefly, no doubt, as one of his biographers explains, the *Heroides* of Ovid ; he may also have known the Epistles of Heloisa, and sentiment of the kind he deals with is common and familiar stuff for all the medieval varieties of courtly poetry. But this does not greatly detract from Boccaccio's originality as an inventor of one of the principal types of the modern novel. The *Filocolo*, his earliest work, is even more remarkable. Boccaccio takes an old French story, one of the best known and one of the most attractive—the story of the true lovers, Floris and Blanchefloure. This he writes out in prose, in his own way, with all the rhetoric, all the classical ornament he can find room for : the result is exactly like one of those Greek rhetorical romances which Boccaccio had never seen, and which were to have such enormous influence two centuries later. The Greek romance of *Theagenes and Chariclea* had, in the sixteenth and the seventeenth century, a value like that of the *Iliad* and the *Aeneid* : Sir Philip Sidney, Tasso, and Cervantes are among the followers of Heliodorus, and speak of him as one of the most honourable names in literature. Boccaccio knew nothing about Heliodorus ; so he invented him. His *Filocolo* is a literary form in which most of the things provided by Heliodorus were anticipated, generations before the Greek romances came to be a power in the West.

The *Ameto* is the first pastoral romance in prose, with poems interspersed,—a form not now much in request, but which was long regarded as an admirable kind of fiction. The catalogue of these romances is a long one ; and though the readers are not many, it is no ignoble company that includes the *Diana* of Montemayor, the *Galatea* of Cervantes, the *Astrée*.

The *Teseide* has a higher eminence in the history of poetry. It is the first attempt, in a modern language, to reproduce the classical epic poem. Boccaccio is the first adventurer in that long line of poets, in all the nations, who have tried for the prize of the epic, " not without dust and heat," and with so many failures, with such vast heaps of wreckage, piles of similes, broken " machines," battered and dingy masks of the gods and goddesses of Olympus ; yet it is not all waste, for *Paradise Lost* is one of the successors of Boccaccio's *Teseide*. *Paradise Lost* was written with the same kind of ambition, to show that the epic forms of the ancients could be reproduced, and filled afresh, by a modern imagination using a modern tongue. *Renaissance* has some meaning as applied to the works of Boccaccio. The contents of the ancient poems had of course never been ignored, and were of as much importance in the twelfth century as in the fourteenth or the sixteenth. But Boccaccio is one of the first of modern writers to try for the form and spirit of classical literature.

He is not absolutely the first, for Dante was before him. Dante was the first to realise the value and the possibilities of the ancient devices in modern poetry ; and some part, not a small part, of Boccaccio's work is to popularise the methods of Dante; for instance in that use of the epic simile which was introduced in English poetry by Chaucer, and which Chaucer learned from Dante and Boccaccio.

The talent of Boccaccio for finding out new kinds of literature, and making the most of them, is like the instinct of a man of business for profitable openings. The works of Boccaccio, other than the *Decameron*, are full of all kinds of faults, from pompous rhetoric to the opposite extreme of mere flatness and negligence ; but nothing impairs his skill in discovering the lines on which he is going to proceed, the ease and security with which he takes up his point of view, decides on his method, and sets to work. The execution may be scamped, may be trivial in one place and emphatic in another, without good reason, but it seldom does much to spoil the good effect of the first design. This intuition of the right lines of a story was what Chaucer learned from Boccaccio. There is nothing more exhilarating in literary history than the way in which Chaucer caught the secret of Boccaccio's work, and used it for his own purposes.

There is more of instinct than of study in Boccaccio's power of designing. He did not sit down, like some later poets, to think about the poetical forms of Greek and Latin poetry, and try to reproduce them. He copied the epic model, it is true, but it does not need much reading to find out that an epic should have a descriptive catalogue of armies, and, if possible, one book of funeral games. The problems of the unities are different from this, and there does not seem to have been anything the least like the theory of the unities in Boccaccio's narrative art, though the narrative unities are there in his compositions. He might say like M. Jourdain : " Cependant je n'ai point étudié, et j'ai fait cela tout du premier coup." He took no pains about the study of classical forms ; his classical researches were of another kind. He liked the matter of ancient learning ; his learned works are encyclopedias ; the *Genealogies of the Gods*, a kind of dictionary of mythology intended for the use of poets, to keep them right in their noble ornamental passages ; *De Casibus Virorum Illustrium* (*The Falls of Princes*, as it is called in the English version, Lydgate's " Bochas ") ; *De Claris Mulieribus* ; and an appendix to the classical dictionary of the gods, providing additional useful information for the poets " concerning Mountains, Woods, Wells, Lakes, Rivers, Pools and Marshes, and concerning the Names of the Sea."

He was not troubled about rhetorical principles, and says nothing much about his art, beyond his explanation of the allegorical theory. His account of Virgil is characteristic. Boccaccio was a professor in his old age ; when he came to Virgil in his Dante lectures he had nothing to tell his audience about Virgil's diction nor about the idea of an Heroic Poem ; he told them that Virgil was an astrologer who lived at Naples, and who made a brazen fly and a bronze horse and the two heads, one weeping and the other laughing, set up at the two sides of the Porta Nolana. But while he neglected the theory of poetical composition he was making discoveries and inventions in literary form, and establishing literary principles in a practical way. He has no criticism in him, but he does more than the work of criticism by the examples he sets. Chaucer, equally without any explicit reflection on the principles of construction, shows how he had made out for himself what Boccaccio was driving at. Chaucer had all the medieval tastes, the taste for exorbitant digressions and irrelevances, the love of useful information, the want of proportion and design. But he read Boccaccio and discovered his secret without any lectures on criticism and without saying much about his discovery. He wrote, in imitation of Boccaccio, the stories of the *Filostrato* and the *Teseide*. He changed them both ; he added substance to Boccaccio's light and graceful form of the story of *Troilus* ; he threw away the epic decorations of *Palamon and Arcita*. In both he retained, from his original, the narrative unity and coherence. How much he learned from Boccaccio, and how little it was in agreement with his own natural proclivities, may be seen in his *House of Fame*. He has just finished his *Troilus and Criseyde*, his greatest work, and one of the greatest imaginative works in English poetry,—a poem which, for sheer strength and firmness of design, not to speak of its other qualities, may stand comparison with anything in the great Elizabethan age, even with Milton himself. When he has finished this piece of work, Chaucer thinks he has earned a holiday, and writes the *House of Fame*—a rambling, unfinished, roundabout paper, with every good old medieval vanity in it—long descriptions, popular scientific lectures, allegories, moralisings, everything that he knew to be wrong, everything that was most familiar and delightful to him from his school-days, and most repugnant to a correct and educated taste. Wherever Chaucer sets himself to do strong work, there is the influence of Boccaccio ; he unbends his mind afterwards, in a plunge among the medieval incongruities ; sometimes with libertine recklessness, as when he imposed the tale of Melibeus on the Canterbury pilgrims ; Melibeus the ineffable, the unlimited, the hopeless embodiment of everything in the Middle Ages most alien to life. The reaction shown in Melibeus may prove how strong the contrary influence was—the lesson of restraint and coherence which Chaucer acquired from Boccaccio.

In his relation to English literature, as the master of Chaucer, Boccaccio may seem to have the character of an academic and scholarly person prescribing rules. This is illusion. Boccaccio had a natural gift for story-telling, and for coherence in story-telling. His talent for composition, design, arrangement, gives him his rank among literary reformers. But this talent remains always natural, and half unconscious. There are pedantries in Boccaccio, but not the academic and formal pedantry of the sixteenth-century literary men. He does not lecture on the principles of composition. He has not Dante's affection for philology ; he would not have had much sympathy for Tasso's painful defences and explanations about the plan and details of his epic.

Boccaccio has his strength from the land of Italy, like Virgil, Horace, and Ovid. He has the old pieties of the country people. The best things in his great classical dictionary are the references to the undying popular beliefs and rituals. Though he did not get on well with his father, he remembers with affection the old religion of the New Year's Eve, when his father used to repeat the old country observance, and pour a libation on the burning log for the gods of the household. In the same temper as Sidney's praise of the ballads, he finds the spirit of poetry in the old wives' fairy tales at the fireside in the winter nights. One of his greatest achievements in poetry, the confirmation of the octave stanza as the Italian heroic measure, is due to his trust in Italian manners and traditions. The *ottava rima* is a popular, not a learned, form of verse. It is not a rude or barbarous measure ; it is ultimately derived no doubt from the courtly schools ; but still it is popular, because the common people of Italy, and more especially of Tuscany, have chosen to make it so. The stanzas of the early popular romances of Tuscany show distinctly their relation to the lyrical form of the *rispetti*, which are to this day, it would seem, the favourite form among the Tuscan villagers. Thus the following example from the *Cantare di Fiorio e Biancifiore*, shows the same device of repetition (*ripresa*) which is obligatory in the lyrical *rispetti* :—

> Alora dise Fiorio : E io vi vo' andare,
> e metere mi voglio per la via,
> e cercaragio la terra e lo mare,
> con tutta quanta la Saracinia ;
> e giamai non credo in quà tornare
> s' io non ritruovo la speranza mia ;
> giamai a voi io non ritorneraggio,
> s' io non riveggio 'l suo chiaro visaggio.

The mode of the *rispetti* is this :—

> Non ti maravigliar se tu sei bella,
> Perchè sei nata accanto alla marina ;
> L' acqua del mar ti mantien fresca e bella
> Come la rosa in sulla verde spina :
> Se delle rose ce n' è nel rosaio,
> Nel tuo viso ci sono di gennaio ;
> Se delle rose nel rosaio ne fosse,
> Nel tuo viso ci sono bianche e rosse.[1]

Boccaccio, in adopting this popular stanza for his romantic and epic verse, was acknowledging his reliance on the genius of the popular poetry. This, together with his command of the vulgar idiom in his prose, gives him his authority in Italian literature at the beginning of the new age. It is the good fortune of Italian poetry that at a time when there was so much danger of pedantry and formalism, of mere classical imitation, Boccaccio was there to set the

---

[1] Tigri, *Canti Popolari Toscani* (1856), p. 15.

force of his example and influence against the encroachments of fanatic precisians. He had too much learning, too strong a faculty for design, too great variety and liveliness of elocution, to be ignored by any scholar. He could not be dismissed as a barbarian ; and he was too ingenuous, too fond of the Tuscan earth, the Tuscan air, to admit the sterile blight of the false classicism. In his own way and degree he did what Catullus and Lucretius, Virgil and Ovid, had done before him—by taking all he could get from the universal sources of learning, while he kept his loyalty to the native genius of Italy. Thus he appears at the beginning of the Renaissance well protected against some of its most insidious vanities,—just as the great Latin poets were saved by the same Italian genius from the dangers of a too absolute subservience to Greece.

CHAUCER

THERE is hardly any author of whom so many commonplaces are true, and by whom so many commonplaces are proved to be inept and ridiculous. The commonplaces of historical origin and environment, of the conditions of literary production, of the evolution of literary forms, and all the rest of them, are verified and illustrated in the life of Chaucer. "The poet as representative of his age" is made ready for the preacher in the volumes of Chaucer. The author of *Typical Developments* might find his booty in those early poems of Chaucer that seem at first to be the product wholly of some "tendency," some "spirit of the age," without any admixture of any particular character from the man who took the trouble to write them. And it is not one tendency only, or one taste or study, that is embodied in Chaucer's writings, but all the ideas, all the prepossessions, all the fashions, all the vanities of the world, from courtly rhyming to importunate moralities; all the learning, from the trivial arts to the heights of Astronomy, and beyond the *primum mobile*. He comes out of the Middle Ages like Glaucus from the sea, in the tenth book of the *Republic*, where the real man, or god, is unrecognisable in the overgrowth of shells and tangle. The rich chaotic and formless life, the ooze and wrack of the medieval depths, are indeed left behind and cleared away when Chaucer comes to his own. But no great poet has retained in so large a part of his extant work the common "form and pressure" of his own time and the generation immediately before his own.

Dante had as large a share of medieval learning, and in his earlier writings is almost as much subject as Chaucer was to the prevalent fashions. There is not, however, in the progress of Dante from the earlier poetical conventions and from the learning of the schools, the same paradoxical element as in the history of Chaucer's poetry. Dante in one way is a "representative" of medieval habits of thought and imagination, shared by him with unnumbered nameless scholars and metaphysical poets. But he always wears the common habit with some difference of his own, and, more than that, he carries up all the commonplaces of his reading and his early experiments into the "heaven of his invention," in the *Divine Comedy*. Whereas Chaucer is again and again content to remain simply on the level of his own time: one large fragment of the *Canterbury Tales* is an undistinguished and unmanageable block of the most hopeless commonplace : the *Tale of Melibeus* is a thing incapable of life, under any process of interpretation, a lump of the most inert "first matter" of medieval pedantry, which is yet introduced by Chaucer in his own person, in company with his latest and finest work, for the entertainment of the Canterbury pilgrims. In many of his poems, though in these always with some grace of form and never with anything like the oppression of Melibeus, Chaucer repeats the common tunes, the idle sequences of phrases and rhymes in fashion among the most abstract and most unsubstantial of all the schools of poetry. In his great poems, in *Troilus*, in the *Legend of Good Women*, in the most notable parts of the *Canterbury Tales*, he has carried on the commonplace matter to a higher form, and has given individuality to the commonplace without destroying its generic character altogether ; as, in his own way, Dante always, in the most exalted parts of his poetry in the *Commedia*, retains some of the features of the *Vita Nuova* and the *Convivio*. Chaucer, however, in his collected writings is encumbered, unlike Dante, with a crowd of miscellaneous pieces of work ; sketches, fragments, translations, exercises, the product of hours in which he had no call to do anything else or anything better than a

journalist or an ordinary person might do. He
could escape, when he thought good, from the
restrictions of the medieval habit ; he could turn
the medieval fashion into something incomparably
bright and lively ; he could give body and strength
to the dreams and the echoes of the garden of the
Rose. But very often, and that to the very end of
his life, he found it easier and more comfortable to
take the traditional conventions as he found them,
and to use them as they were used by people of
no importance and no remarkable power of their
own.

It is this relation of Chaucer to the medieval
commonplaces that gives room for any amount of
historical commentary. Mr. Lowell asks, at the
beginning of his essay, " Will it *do* to say anything
more about Chaucer ? Can any one hope to say
anything, not new, but even fresh, on a topic so
well-worn ? " It is no less fair a problem to inquire
whether there can ever be any end to the illustration of a writer who is in such sympathy with the
common moods of his contemporaries and his predecessors that every new discovery or new opinion
about the literary wealth of the Middle Ages must
inevitably have some bearing, more or less direct, on
the study of his writings. It is still a long way to
the end, and not so very far from the beginning of
the criticism of the French poets whom Chaucer

read. It is only the other day that the poems of
Oton de Granson were discovered,—" Graunson flour
of hem that maken in France,"—and among them the
original of Chaucer's *Complaint of Venus*. There is
not yet any good edition of Machault, and the
edition of Eustache Deschamps is not yet completed
for the Société des anciens Textes.[1] It is still open to
any one to make his own critical judgment of the
works of those authors ; there has been little dicta-
tion of any formal or established opinion on the
subject. Those authors are included in the great
host of amatory poets whose common qualities are so
common, and whose distinctive characters are so hard
to fix and to describe. Little has yet been done to
seize the volatile essence of that courtly poetry which
takes so many forms in different countries, and all of
them so shadowy. So long as the spirit of those
French poets is still undetected and undescribed,
except in the most general terms, by the literary
historian, it cannot be said that the criticism of
Chaucer is exhausted.

It is easily possible to be tired of the historical
criticism that plies its formulas over the sources and
origins of poetry, and attempts to work out the
spiritual pedigree of a genius. It cannot, however,
be seriously argued that inquiries of this sort are
inept in the case of Chaucer, whose obligations to his

[1] Written in 1895 : the edition was finished (11 volumes) in 1903.

ancestors are manifest in every page, not to speak of those debts that are less obvious. If the result, in most instances, is to bring out Chaucer's independence more in relief by the subtraction of his loans, and to prove the limitations of this historical method when it is made to confront the problems of original and underived imagination, there is no great harm done, but the contrary. It is the result to be looked for.

With one of Chaucer's poems the inquiry into origins has scored a conspicuous success, and in an equal degree has found its limits and proved its inability, after all, to analyse the inexplicable. The *House of Fame* has been subjected to laborious study, and one important set of facts has been brought to evidence about it. The relation of the poem to the *Divine Comedy* has been considered and discussed by Sandras, Ten Brink, Mr. Skeat, and other scholars. The proof is decisive. There is no remnant of doubt that Chaucer had been reading Dante when he wrote the *House of Fame*; that he derived from the suggestions of Dante the images and the pageants of his dream, and many of the phrases in which it is narrated. Here, however, the proof comes to an end. The historical inquiry can do no more. And when all is said and done, the *House of Fame* still stands where it stood—a poem inexplicable by any references to the poem from which it was borrowed—

G

a poem as different from the *Divine Comedy* as it is possible to find in any Christian tongue. The true criticism of the poem has to begin where the historical apparatus leaves off. If its quiddity is to be extracted, the *House of Fame* must be taken, first of all, as the poem it is, not as the poem from which it is derived.

It is in this way that the works of Chaucer afford the most delightful tests of ingenuity and of the validity and right use of the methods of criticism. No task is more dangerous for a critic who has his own private device for the solution of all problems. The problems in Chaucer are continually altering, and the ground is one that calls for all varieties of skill if it is to be tracked out and surveyed in all its changes of level.

The *Canterbury Tales*, which include so much, do not include the whole of Chaucer. Some of his masterpieces are there, and there is nothing like the Prologue anywhere else ; but outside of the group of the Tales is to be found the finest work of Chaucer in the more abstract and delicate kind of poetry, *Anelida* ; the most massive and the richest of his compositions, which is *Troilus* ; and the most enthralling and most musical of all his idylls, in the Prologue to the *Legend of Good Women*, with the balade of Alcestis, " sung in carolwise " :

Hyd, Absolon, thy gilte tresses clere.

The poem of *Anelida and the False Arcite*, it may be suspected, is too often and too rashly passed over. It has a good deal of the artificial and exquisite qualities of the court poetry ; it appears to be wanting in substance. Yet for that very reason the fineness of the style in this unfinished poetical essay gives it rank among the greater poems, to prove what elegance might be attained by the strong hand of the artist, when he chose to work in a small scale. Further, and apart from the elaboration of the style, the poem is Chaucer's example of the abstract way of story-telling. It is the light ghost of a story, the antenatal soul of a substantial poem. The characters are merely types, the situation is a mathematical theorem ; yet this abstract drama, of the faithless knight who leaves his true love for the sake of a wanton shrew, is played as admirably, in its own way, as the history of the two Noble Kinsmen, or the still nobler Troilus.

It is difficult to speak temperately of Chaucer's *Troilus*. It is the first great modern book in that kind where the most characteristic modern triumphs of the literary art have been won—in the kind to which belong the great books of Cervantes, of Fielding, and of their later pupils,—that form of story which is not restricted in its matter in any way, but is capable of taking in comprehensively all or any part of the aspects and humours of life. No other medieval poem is rich and full in the same way as *Troilus* is full of varieties of character and mood. It is a tragic novel, and it is also strong enough to pass the scrutiny of that Comic Muse who detects the impostures of inflated heroic and romantic poetry. More than this, it has the effective aid of the Comic Muse in that alliance of tragedy and comedy which makes an end of all the old distinctions and limitations of narrative and drama.

The original of *Troilus*, the *Filostrato* of Boccaccio, is scarcely more substantial in its dramatic part, though it is longer and has a more elaborate plot, than Chaucer's *Anelida*. The three personages of the one poem are not more definite than the three of the other. The *Filostrato* is not merely "done into English" in Chaucer's *Troilus and Criseyde*. Chaucer has done much more than that for the original poem ; he has translated it from one form of art into another,—from the form of a light romantic melody, vague and graceful, into the form of a story of human characters, and of characters strongly contrasted and subtly understood by the author. The difference is hardly less than that between the Italian novels and the English tragedies of *Romeo* or *Othello*, as far at least as the representation of character is concerned. Chaucer learned from Boccaccio the art of construction : the design of the *Filostrato* is, in the main outline, the design of

Chaucer's *Troilus and Criseyde* ; but in working out
his story of these " tragic comedians," the English
poet has taken his own way—a way in which he had
no forerunners that he knew of, and for successors
all the dramatists and novelists of all the modern
tongues.

No other work of Chaucer's has the same dignity
or the same commanding beauty. It would be
difficult to find in any language, in any of the
thousand experiments of the modern schools of
novelists, a story so perfectly proportioned and composed—a method of narrative so completely adequate.
Of the dramatic capacities of the original plot, considering the use made of it in Shakespeare's *Troilus
and Cressida*, there is little need to say anything.
Boccaccio chose and shaped the plot of his story with
absolute confidence and success : there is nothing to
break the outline. The general outline is kept by
Chaucer, who thus obtains for his story a plan compared with which the plan of Fielding's greatest novel
is ill-devised, awkward, and irregular ; while the
symmetry and unity of Chaucer's story are compatible
with a leisure and a profusion in the details not less
than Shakespeare's, and in this case more suitably
bestowed than in Shakespeare's *Troilus.* There is
nothing in the art of any narrative more beautiful
than Chaucer's rendering of the uncertain, faltering,
and transient moods that go to make the graceful

and mutable soul of Cressida ; nothing more perfect in its conception and its style than his way of rendering the suspense of Troilus ; the slowly rising doubt and despair keeping pace in the mind of Troilus with the equally gradual and inevitable withdrawal and alteration of love in the mind of his lady, till he comes to the end of his love-story in Cressida's weak and helpless letter of defence and deprecation.

Besides the triumph of art in the representation of the characters, there are more subsidiary beauties in *Troilus* than anywhere else in Chaucer—as in the effective details of the less important scenes, the ladies reading the romance of Thebes together, the amateur medical advice for the fever of Troilus, the visit of Helen the queen, the very Helen of the *Odyssey*, to show kindness to Troilus in his sickness. There are other poems of Chaucer—the *Knight's Tale* for instance—in which Chaucer relies more consistently throughout on the spell of pure romance, without much effort at strong dramatic composition. But it is in *Troilus*, where the art of Chaucer was set to do all its utmost in the fuller dramatic form of story, that the finest passages of pure romance are also to be found,—in *Troilus*, and not in the story of Palamon and Arcite, or of Constance, or of Cambuscan, or any other. At least it may be imagined that few readers who remember the most memorable passage of pure narrative in *Troilus*,—his entrance into Troy from the battle without,—will be inclined to dispute the place of honour given to it by Chaucer's last disciple, in his profession of allegiance in the *Life and Death of Jason*. The "tragedie" of the lovers is embellished with single jewels more than can be easily reckoned ; with scenes and pictures of pure romance ; with the humours and the "ensamples" and opinions of Pandarus ; with verses of pure melody, that seem to have caught beforehand all the music of Spenser :

> And as the newe abaysshed nightingale
> That stinteth first whan she biginnith singe ;

with many other passages from which the reader receives the indefinable surprise that is never exhausted by long acquaintance, and that makes the reader know he is in the presence of one of the adepts. But all these single and separable beauties are nothing in comparison with the organic and structural beauty of the poem, in the order of its story, and in the life of its personages.

Chaucer is always at his best when he is put on his mettle by Boccaccio. He is well enough content in other instances to borrow a story ready-made. In his appropriation of Boccaccio he is compelled by his sense of honour to make something as good if he can, in a way of his own. He learns from the Italian the lesson of sure and definite exposition ; he does not

copy the Italian details or the special rhetorical prescriptions. The story of *Palamon and Arcite*, on
which Chaucer appears to have spent so much of his
time, is a different sort of thing from *Troilus* ; the
problems are different ; the result is no less fortunate
in its own way. The *Teseide*, the original of the
Knight's Tale, is reduced in compass under Chaucer's
treatment, as much as the *Filostrato* is strengthened
and enlarged. The *Teseide*, unlike the *Filostrato*, is
an ambitious experiment, no less than the first poem
in the solemn procession of modern epics according
to the rules of the ancients,—an epic poem written
correctly, in twelve books, with epic similes, Olympian
machinery, funeral games, and a catalogue of the
forces sent into the field—all according to the best
examples. Chaucer brings it down to the form of
a romance, restoring it, no doubt, to the form of
Boccaccio's lost original, whatever that may have
been ; at any rate to the common scale of the less
involved and less extravagant among the French
romances of the twelfth or thirteenth century. For
Boccaccio's *Theseid*, with all its brilliance, is somewhat
tedious, as an epic poem may be ; it is obviously out
of condition, and overburdened in its heroic accoutre-
ments. The *Knight's Tale* is well designed, and
nothing in it is superfluous. There are some well-
known instances in it of the success with which
Chaucer has changed the original design : reducing

the pompous and unwieldy epic catalogue of heroes
to the two famous contrasted pictures "in the Gothic
manner," the descriptions of Lycurgus and Emetreus,
and rejecting Boccaccio's awkward fiction in the
account of the prayers of Palamon, Arcita, and
Emilia. But the most significant part of Chaucer's
work in this story is the deliberate evasion of anything like the drama of *Troilus and Cressida*.

The *Knight's Tale* is a romance and nothing more
—a poem, a story, in which the story and the melody
of the poem are more than the personages. Chaucer
saw that the story would not bear a strong dramatic
treatment. The Comic Muse was not to be bribed :
neither then, nor later, when the rash experiment
of Fletcher in the *Two Noble Kinsmen* proved how
well the elder poet was justified in refusing to give
this story anything like the burden of *Troilus*. The
Lady Emilia, most worshipful and most shadowy
lady in the romance, is too cruelly put to the ordeal
of tragedy : the story is refuted as soon as it is made
to bear the weight of tragic passion or thought.
Chaucer, who found the story of *Troilus* capable of
bearing the whole strength of his genius, deals gently
with the fable of the *Theseid* : the characters are not
brought forward ; instead of the drama of *Troilus*,
there is a sequence of pictures ; the landscapes of
romance, the castles and the gardens, are more than
the figures that seem to move about among them.

There is pathos in the *Knight's Tale*, but there is
no true tragedy. How admirably Chaucer tells the
pathetic story may be seen at once by comparing the
meeting of Palamon and Arcite in the wood with the
corresponding scene in Fletcher's play :—

> Ther nas no good day, ne no saluing ;
> But streight, withouten word or rehersing,
> Everich of hem halp for to armen other,
> As freendly as he were his owne brother.

This simplicity of style is the perfection of mere
narrative, as distinguished from the higher and more
elaborate forms of epic poetry or prose. The situation here rendered is one that does not call for any
dramatic fulness or particularity : the characters of
Palamon and Arcite in any case are little qualified
for impressive drama. But the pathos of the meeting, and of the courtesy rendered to one another by
the two friends in their estrangement, is a pathos
almost wholly independent of any delineation of their
characters. The characters are nothing : it is " any
friend to any friend," an abstract formula, used by
Chaucer in this place with an art for which he found
no suggestion in Boccaccio, nor obtained any recog-
nition from Fletcher. In the *Teseide* the rivals meet
and argue with one another before the duel in which
they are interrupted by Theseus ; in the play of the
Two Noble Kinsmen they converse without any
apparent strain. In Chaucer's poem the division

between them is made deeper, and indicated with greater effect in four lines, than in the eloquence of his Italian master or his English pupil.

Such is the art of Chaucer in the *Knight's Tale* : perfect in its own kind, but that kind not the greatest. It needs the infinitely stronger fable of his *Troilus and Criseyde* to bring out the strength of his imagination. *Troilus*, to use a familiar term of Chaucer's own, cannot but " distain " by comparison the best of the *Canterbury Tales*. *Troilus* is not a romance, but a dramatic story, in which the characters speak for themselves, in which the elements that in the *Canterbury Tales* are dissipated or distributed among a number of tales and interludes are all brought together and made to contribute in due proportion to the total effect of the poem. In the *Canterbury Tales* the comic drama is to be found at its best outside of the stories—best of all in the dramatic monologues of the *Wife of Bath* and the *Pardoner*. It takes nothing away from the glory of those dramatic idylls to maintain that Chaucer's Pandarus belongs to a higher and more difficult form of comic imagination. The *Wife of Bath* and the *Pardoner* are left to themselves as much, or very nearly as much, as the *Northern Farmer* or *Mr. Sludge the Medium*. Pandarus has to acquit himself as well as he may on the same stage as other and more tragic personages, in a story where there are other interests besides that of his humour and his proverbial philosophy. This is not a question of tastes and preferences, but a question of the distinction between different kinds and varieties of narrative poetry. It is open to any one to have any opinion he pleases about the value of Chaucer's poetry. But the question of value is one thing : the question of kinds is another. The value may be disputed indefinitely : the kind may be ascertained and proved. The kind of poetry to which *Troilus* belongs is manifestly different from that of each and all of the *Canterbury Tales*, and manifestly a richer and more fruitful kind ; and for this reason alone the poem of *Troilus* would stand out from among all the other poems of its author.

The problems regarding Chaucer's methods of composition are inexhaustible. They are forced on the attention, naturally, by Mr. Skeat's edition of his writings, in which the contradictions and paradoxes of Chaucer's life appear more obvious and striking than they ever were before. *Boece* and *Troilus*, which are mentioned together by Chaucer himself, are here associated in the same volume : the *Treatise on the Astrolabe* goes along with the *Legend of Good Women*. Of all the critical problems offered by this great collection of the works of a great master there is none more fascinating and none more hopeless than the task of following his changes of mood and his changes of handling. *Troilus* is followed by the *House of Fame*—a caprice, a fantasy, the poet's compensation to himself for the restraint and the application bestowed on his greater poem. "Ne jompre eek no discordant thing yfere" is the advice of a literary critic in the book of *Troilus* itself: the critic knew the medieval temptation to drag in "termes of physik" and other natural sciences, whether they were required or not. The *House of Fame* is an indulgence, after *Troilus*, in all the medieval vanities that had been discouraged by the ambitious and lordly design of that poem. Allegory, description, painted walls, irrelevant science, pageants and processions of different kinds, everything that the average medieval book makes play with,—these are the furniture of the *House of Fame*; and, in addition to these and through all these, there is the irony of the dream, and the humorous self-depreciation which gives to the *House of Fame* the character of a personal confession. It is one of the most intimate as well as one of the most casual of all his works,—a rambling essay in which all the author's weaknesses of taste are revealed, all his fondness for conformity with his age and its manners, while at the same time there is no other poem of Chaucer's so clear and so ironical in its expression of his own view of himself. On the one hand, it is related to all the dreariest and stalest medieval fashions; on the other, to the

liveliest moods of humorous literature. The temper
of Chaucer in his tedious description of the pictures
from the *Æneid*, in the first book, is in accord
with all the most monotonous and drawling poets of
the medieval schools ; his wit in the colloquy with
the eagle in the second book is something hardly to
be matched except in literature outside the medieval
conventions altogether. The disillusion of the poet,
when he imagines that he is going to heaven to be
" stellified," and is undeceived by his guide, is like
nothing in the world so much as the conversation
with Poseidon in Heine's *Nordsee*, where the voyager
has his fears removed in a manner equally patronising
and uncomplimentary.

The contradictions and the problems of the *House
of Fame*, in respect of its composition and its poetical
elements, are merely those that are found still more
profusely and more obviously in the *Canterbury Tales*.
There is little need for anyone to say more than
Dryden has said, or to repeat what every reader can
find out for himself, about the liveliness of the livelier
parts of the collection. The Prologue, the Interludes
of conversation and debate, the Host's too masterful
good humour, the considerate and gentle demeanour
of the Monk, the Shipman's defence of true religion,
the confessions of the Wife of Bath and the Pardoner,
the opinions of the Canon's Yeoman,—of all this,
and of everything of this sort in the book, it is

hopeless to look for any terms of praise that will not sound superfluous to people with eyes and wits of their own. It is not quite so irrelevant to inquire into the nature of the separate tales, and to ask how it is that so many of them have so little of the character of Chaucer, if Chaucer is to be judged by the Prologue and the Interludes.

Some of the Tales are early works, and that explains something of the mystery. Still the fact remains that those early works were adopted and ratified by Chaucer in the composition of his great work, when he made room for the Life of St. Cecilia, and expressly set himself to bespeak an audience for the gravity of *Melibeus*. Here again, though on a still larger scale, is the contradiction of the elements of the *House of Fame*, the discord between the outworn garment of the Middle Ages and the new web from which it is patched.

There is nothing in all the *Canterbury Tales* to set against the richly varied story of *Troilus and Criseyde*. There are, however, certain of the *Canterbury Tales* which are not less admirable in respect of mere technical beauty of construction, though the artistic skill is not shown in the same material as in *Troilus*. The *Knight's Tale* preserves the epic, or rather the romantic unities of narrative, as admirably as the greater poem. The *Nun's Priest's Tale* is equally perfect in its own way, and that way is one in which

Chaucer has no rival. The story of Virginia, the story of the fairy bride, the story of the revellers who went to look for Death, and many others, are planned without weakness or hesitation in the design. There are others which have an incurable fault in construction, a congenital weakness, utterly at variance from the habit of Chaucer as shown elsewhere, and from the critical principles which he had clearly mastered for his own guidance in his study of Boccaccio.

The *Man of Law's Tale*, the story of Constance, is a comparatively early work, which Chaucer apparently did not choose to alter as he altered his first version of *Palamon and Arcite*. At any rate, the story declares itself as part of a different literary tradition from those in which Chaucer has taken his own way with the proportions of the narrative. The story of Constance has hardly its equal anywhere for nobility of temper ; but in respect of unity and harmony of design it is as weak and uncertain as the *Knight's Tale* is complete, continuous, and strong. Chaucer, whose modifications of Boccaccio are proof of intense critical study and calculation of the dimensions of his stories, here admits, to rank with his finished work, a poem beautiful for everything except those constructive excellences on which he had come to set so much account in other cases. The story of Constance follows the lines of a dull original. It has the defects, or rather the excesses, of most

popular traditional fairy-tales. Chaucer, who afterwards refused to translate Boccaccio literally, here
follows closely the ill-designed plot of a writer who
was not in the least like Boccaccio. The story
repeats twice over, with variations in detail, the adventure of the princess suffering from the treacherous
malice of a wicked mother-in-law ; and, also twice
over, her voyage in a rudderless boat ; the incident
of her deliverance from a villain, the Northumbrian
caitiff in the first instance, the heathen lord's steward
in the second, is also repeated ; while the machinery
of the first false charge made against Constance by
the Northumbrian adversary goes some way to spoil
the effect of the subsequent false charge made by
the queen-mother, Donegild. The poem has beauties
enough to make any one ashamed of criticism ; yet
it cannot be denied that its beauties are often the
exact opposite of the virtues of Chaucer's finished
work, being beauties of detail and not beauties of
principle and design. The *Man of Law's Tale* with
all the grace of Chaucer's style has also the characteristic unwieldiness of the common medieval
romance ; while the *Knight's Tale*, which is no finer
in details, is as a composition finished and coherent,
with no unnecessary or irrelevant passages.

Besides the anomalies of construction in the
Canterbury Tales, and not less remarkable than the
difference between the neatness and symmetry of

H

the *Knight's Tale* and the flaccidity of the *Man of Law's*, there is an anomaly of sentiment and of mood. *Melibeus* may be left out of account, as a portent too wonderful for mortal commentary : there are other problems and distresses in the *Canterbury Tales*, and they are singular enough, though not altogether inexplicable or " out of all whooping," like that insinuating " little thing in prose " by which Sir Thopas was avenged on his detractors.

The *Knight's Tale* is an artifice, wholly successful, but not to be tampered with in any way, and above all things not to be made into a drama, except for the theatre of the mind. Chaucer refused to give to Emilie and her rival lovers one single spark of that imaginative life which makes his story of *Troilus* one of the great narrative poems of the world, without fear of comparison with the greatest stories in verse or prose. By the original conception of the *Knight's Tale*, the Lady Emilie is forbidden to take any principal part in the story. This is an initial fallacy, a want of dramatic proportion, which renders the plot impossible for the strongest forms of novel or of tragedy. But Chaucer saw that the fable, too weak, too false for the stronger kind, was exactly right when treated in the fainter kind of narrative which may be called romance, or by any other name that will distinguish it from the order of *Troilus*, from the stronger kind of story in which the characters are true.

In some of the other Tales the experiment is more hazardous, the success not quite so admirable. What is to be said of the *Clerk's Tale* ? what of the *Franklin's* ? That the story of Griselda should have been chosen by the author of *Troilus* for an honourable place in his *Canterbury Tales* is almost as pleasant as the publication of *Persiles and Sigismunda* by the author of *Don Quixote*. Chaucer had good authority for the patience of Griselda ; by no author has the old story been more beautifully and pathetically rendered, and his *Envoy* saves him from the suspicion of too great solemnity : but no consideration will ever make up for the disparity between the monotonous theme and the variety of Chaucer's greater work—between this formal virtue of the pulpit and the humanities outside. In the *Franklin's Tale* again, in a different way, Chaucer has committed himself to superstitions of which there is no vestige in the more complex parts of his poetry. As Griselda represents the abstract and rectilinear virtue of medieval homilists, the *Franklin's Tale* revolves about the point of honour, no less gallantly than Prince Prettyman in the *Rehearsal*. The virtue of patience, the virtue of truth, are there impaled, crying out for some gentle casuist to come and put them out of their torment. Many are the similar victims, from Sir Amadace to Hernani : "the horn of the old Gentleman" has compelled innumerable romantic

heroes to take unpleasant resolutions for the sake of
a theatrical effect. That the point of honour, the
romantic tension between two abstract opposites,
should appear in Chaucer, the first of modern poets
to give a large, complete, and humorous representation of human action, is merely one of the many
surprises which his readers have to accept as best
they may. It is only one of his thousand and one
caprices : the only dangerous mistake to which it
could possibly lead would be an assumption that the
Franklin's Tale can stand as a sample of Chaucer's
art in its fullest expression ; and the danger of such
an error is small. The beginning of right acquaintance with Chaucer is the conviction that nothing
represents him except the whole body of his writings.
So one is brought round to Dryden's comfortable
and sufficient formula : "Here is God's plenty."
From the energy and the volume of his Trojan story,
as glorious as his Trojan river :

> And thou, Simoys, that as an arwe clere
> Through Troie rennest ay downward to the se ;

from the passion and the music of that "tragedie"
to the doleful voices of *Melibeus*, there is no form
or mood, no fashion of all the vanities, that is not
in some way or other represented there.

GOWER.

GOWER has not lacked praise in his day ; few authors have a better record. To be ranked along with Chaucer, "superlative as poets laureate," to receive, along with Chaucer, the homage of all the notable English and Scottish poets for more than a century, and still to be remembered with esteem in the days of Shakespeare—this is the reward of Gower's learning and diligence. Naturally there is much to set off on the other side. If he was equalled with Chaucer, so was Lydgate, as in Dunbar's *Lament for the Makers*, speaking of the triumph of Death,

> He has done peteouslie devour
> The noble Chaucer of makaris flour,
> The Monk of Bery and Gower all thre.

And the fame of Gower, which from the first had something conventional and fashionable about it, became more and more shadowy, till at last his reputation settled down into a place merely respectable in the history of English literature, as a sort of foil to Chaucer. He is taken to represent the ideals and the learning of Chaucer without his genius ; he is the average educated man of the fourteenth century at his best, brought by training and industry to the accomplishment of a large amount of literary work, but essentially commonplace and dull for all his polite literature.   Such, it may be said, is the established opinion about Gower, where he is remembered at all.

Before Mr. Macaulay's,[1] there was no complete edition of Gower.   His English book, the *Confesssio Amantis*, had never been well edited ; his French book, the *Speculum Meditantis*, was lost.   Mr. Macaulay has discovered the *Speculum Meditantis* ; he has made a good text of the English poem. These are the chief things.   It is something to have found a lost work of an old English poet, in a language so interesting historically as Gower's French ; and the text of the *Confessio Amantis* needed revision as much as anything in the documents of that time.   Besides, Mr. Macaulay has given the Latin poems and the French *balades* of Gower, and provided for all his matter a thoroughly sound apparatus of history, philology, and criticism. Few books are easier to review ; everything that can be wanted has been foreseen.   It is a pleasure to

[1] *The Complete Works of John Gower.*   Edited from the Manuscripts, with Introductions, Notes, and Glossaries.   By G. C. Macaulay.   Four vols.   Oxford : Clarendon Press, 1899-1902.

look at Mr. Macaulay's workmanship. He has
mastered his subject; he has not grudged the most
laborious scrutiny of details;[1] and his good sense
and discretion are shown equally in explaining his
author's grammar, in deciding on the text, and in
estimating the value of the poetry.

That Mr. Macaulay's judgment is to be trusted
on points of taste has been shown in his little book
on Francis Beaumont (1883). In dealing with
Gower he has been compelled to turn to many things
less attractive than the purely literary criticism of his
author; he has proved that good sense in one
department of literature is no disqualification for
other kinds of study; and though he has probably
less liking for philological investigation than for the
historical point of view, he gives the same steady
attention to both. The old allegory of the wedding
of Mercury and Philology has been too often belied
by numerous relations of the lady; it is satisfactory
to find the parties, Wit and Learning, so well
reconciled as here.

The new edition will make no revolutionary
change in the general estimate of Gower. He
remains what he was before, in the common opinion

---

[1] One curious point is decided by Mr. Macaulay. Why does Gower
refer to "Civile" (the civil law) as authority for the fable of the "Dog
in the Manger"? Because the "Lex Furia Caninia" had been repealed
as *invida*, and was generally misconstrued as "Lex Canina." (See the
note on *Conf. Amant.* ii. 83.)

of most critics—an industrious and fluent writer,
a steady moralist, fully possessed of all the available doctrine, and all the usual illustrations and
examples, that were at the service of any preacher.
Mr. Macaulay, by his discovery of a large new
portion of the works of Gower, has even done something to deepen the impression that Gower's talent
is commonplace; for the *Speculum Meditantis*,
the *Mirour de l'Omme*, contains thirty thousand
lines of flat moralising, every page of it full of
the things that every one knew, a mirror of the
medieval doctrine which belonged to no one in
particular.

At the same time, without any paradox or any
attempt to find unappreciated genius in Gower, Mr.
Macaulay's remarks on his literary character have
brought out more clearly the very considerable merit
of his style; and the result is that Gower, though
somewhat heavily weighted with the addition of
his long French poem, comes out with increased
distinction as a "correct" poet. "Correctness"
is his poetical virtue, his title of honour. It has
been recognised before; but in the newly established
text of the *Confessio Amantis* the art of Gower is
shown to have been greater than was supposed when
his text was still troubled with small inaccuracies.
Now it has been restored and burnished; and
Gower, in spite of all his heavy matter, appears as a

poet with a distinct and individual grace, still to be
read with pleasure. The spirit of poetry has seldom
had to contend with so large a mass of prose as the
contents of Gower's moral encyclopedias, but it has
not been defeated. It is hardly discernible in Gower
except in the ease of his style ; but this is in its way
as truly poetical as the stronger powers of imagination or lyric passion, which Gower did not possess.
It may seem a slender gift when compared with the
wealth of Chaucer, but it is no less sincere and true.
He takes the ear with his unaffected flowing verse ;
it steals into the mind before the art of it is consciously noted, " the sense variously drawn out from
one line to another," the accents varied in a way that
has become traditional in English short verse of this
kind. Apart from the ancient language, Gower's
melody is that of modern English poetry, or rather
of no particular age at all.

> Bot for men sein, and soth it is,
> That who that al of wisdom writ
> It dulleth ofte a mannes wit
> To him that schal it aldai rede,
> For thilke cause, if that ye rede,
> I wolde go the middel weie,
> And wryte a bok betwen the tweie,
> Somwhat of lust, somwhat of lore,
> That of the lasse or of the more
> Som man mai lyke of that I wryte :
> And for that fewe men endite
> In oure englissch, I thenke make

> A bok for king Richardes sake,
> To whom belongeth my ligeance
> With al myn hertes obeissance
> In al that evere a liege man
> Unto his king may doon or can.

The " progress of poesy " since these lines were written has been in anything but a straight course, and many great and many prosperous poets have come short of the point reached by Gower's style. Who has a right to say that Gower is quaint, or even " medieval " ? Spenser is less secure than Gower ; most of the Elizabethans are loud and affected compared with him. As to the good taste of the eighteenth century, it is perhaps enough to say that it is something different from the courtesy of Chaucer's time ; in poetry it allowed some things which to Gower would have seemed violent. Is Gower more antiquated in style than Dr. Young ? Which is nearer the centre—the passage just quoted, or the following from the moralist of Queen Anne's reign, versifying the Day of Judgment ?

> Now charnels rattle ; scatter'd limbs, and all
> The various bones, obsequious to the call,
> Self mov'd, advance ; the neck, perhaps, to meet
> The distant head ; the distant legs the feet.
> Dreadful to view, see through the dusky sky
> Fragments of bodies in confusion fly,
> To distant regions journeying, there to claim
> Deserted members and compleat the frame.

There is nothing unreasonable in the opinion,

which seems naturally suggested by these invidious comparisons, that Gower had a quality of style for which there is no better term than "natural." It is an old fallacious term in criticism, but it expresses what people mean. Gower "followed Nature," inasmuch as he did not overload, or bluster, or, at any rate in his English work, go raking for ornamental phrases out of books. Like Chaucer's Franklin, he cared nothing for "Marcus, Tullius ne Cithero." [1]

> Colours of rethoryk ben me to queynte.

But his natural utterance is the result of a long process, in which the study of rhetoric had its place, during the generations that formed the courteous art of poetry in France. The beauty of it was that the rhetoric had been thoroughly assimilated and the school processes forgotten before Gower took in hand to write. Young's contemporaries were most of them still conscious of their lessons and anxious to do what the grammar schools had taught them. Gower's language is never strained, and it is never anything but gentle. Wordsworth's ideal of poetical expression might be exemplified from Gower, and justified ; for though Gower's vocabulary is not taken from the

---

[1] Gower really thought there were two of them :

> And thilke time at Rome also
> Was Tullius with Cithero.—*C.A.* iv. 2647.

"humble and rustic life" which Wordsworth recommended, it is natural and unaffected; there is no artificial rhetoric in his phrasing, there are no ornamental words daubed over his page; there is, in short, nothing remarkable about his diction. It is attractive purely through its simplicity and ease, "as clean as hill-well water."

Gower invented nothing, either in style or matter. The merit of his style is that it accomplishes in English what had been attained long before and practised for many generations in France. He belongs to the French courtly school. Everything that is said in praise of Gower's style might be repeated with little variation about many French poets from the twelfth century downward—Benoit de Sainte-More, Chrestien de Troyes and his followers; the authors of the *Romaunt of the Rose* in the thirteenth century; Eustache Deschamps and Froissart, Gower's contemporaries. It was in France, and especially in French short verse, that the style was first employed which Chaucer and Gower made their own in English. It is all French: the simple eloquence, utterly incapable of forced language, utterly different from the old English standard of poetical expression, which still survived in Gower's day in the emphatic splendours of the alliterative poems. It is this quality of style, this perfect ease and freshness, that makes old French literature what it is—a land of rest and solace, where nothing glares, nothing dazzles or stuns the sense,—where the weary reading man may escape from the thunderings and trumpetings of more vehement literary schools.

It was to this that English literature was drawn, from a time long before Gower and Chaucer ; not, indeed, in any unanimous way (otherwise nothing would have remained for Gower to do), but occasionally, tentatively, in the works of writers who kept themselves from the ordinary English faults of misrule and awkwardness, and followed the French example of a proper literary demeanour. Particularly in one poem of the thirteenth century, *The Owl and the Nightingale* (noted by Mr. Macaulay in one place on account of its versification), the new model seems to have been studied, with full appreciation of its meaning and value, in the same original and free way that Chaucer followed in his transactions with foreign literature. *The Owl and the Nightingale* is a humorous poem, written in octosyllabic verse as correct as Chaucer's, with the same ironical self-possession, the same urbanity. Here evidently the phrasing and versification, the correct, unimpeded, fluent style, the poetical good manners, are due to a close knowledge of French literature, and to something more than a mere copying of the external features.

Nicholas of Guildford, the author of *The Owl and the Nightingale*, understood the intentions of the

French authors as Chaucer or, we might say, changing the reference, as Dryden understood them. He was in sympathy with them before he copied their style ; which means that, so early as the thirteenth century, it was possible for an Englishman to compete in English with the elegances of French courtly verse ; to escape, on the one hand, from the hindrances of the common boorish doggerel ; to refuse, on the other, the temptations of the nobler alliterative poetry, and to begin a tradition of polite literature, after the mode of France, without any slavish subjection to the foreigner.

Again, the style of Barbour, though less correct than his contemporary, Gower, proves how well the spirit and manner of France had been appropriated. *The Bruce* is a poem of the same kind as the French life of William Marshall ; in verse, in grammar and diction, it follows the French school ; it has the same simplicity of language, the same ease of narrative as the *Roman de Thèbes* or any other of the romances that Barbour loved.

Chaucer, being a man of genius, made much more than Gower out of his study of his masters ; but Gower, by the side of Chaucer, shows that there was something in the time which encouraged the art of poetry. The end of the fourteenth century saw the culmination of a long process. The correct verse of Chaucer and Gower was required by the conditions

of the age in which they lived ; or, to put it more
positively, they followed a number of early writers
who had tried for correctness, and they were obliged
to try harder and gain more.

The decline of English poetry in the fifteenth
century, with the shambling verse of Lydgate and
the other degenerate Chaucerians, is difficult to
understand and explain. Whatever the cause may
have been, Lydgate, at any rate, serves to bring out
the value of Gower and to mark the period of 1400,
the age of Chaucer, as a time of cultivated literary
taste in which Chaucer was not alone. The latter
half of the fourteenth century is more consciously
artistic, more secure in command of its resources,
than any other period till the time of Pope ; and it
may be doubted whether even Pope is more of an
artist than Gower.

" The spirit of the age " is rightly regarded with
some diffidence by most sober readers when brought
forward to explain any particular facts in literary or
any other history ; but that is no reason why one
should refuse to acknowledge the "general tendencies"
of an historical period. The fourteenth century has
a distinct character, peculiarly interesting as coming
between the medieval and the modern world, not
merely in the hackneyed part of "an age of
transition," but as achieving certain things which no
later progress has surpassed, such as the Chronicles of

Froissart, the prose of Boccaccio, the poems of Dante, Petrarch, and Chaucer. The Italian authors do not concern Gower ; but he is pretty fully in sympathy with Froissart, and shares with him the characteristic fourteenth-century habit of mind.

The fourteenth century was too late for that medieval ferment of invention and exploration, that great romantic movement which, in the twelfth century, had discovered and put into shape an infinity of stories for the whole of Christendom to enjoy and to repeat ; all the old "matters of Rome and of Britain," the tales of Troy and of Thebes, of Arthur and Alexander. In the fourteenth there was not much to be done in the way of new subject-matter, except in contemporary history, like Froissart's. The artists, like Boccaccio and Chaucer, were chiefly engaged in recasting old material, with a definite resolve to make the form expressive and valuable for its own sake. Literary reflection and criticism (though these had not been wanting in the earlier days among the French and Provençal poets) were now more self-conscious and ambitious. The artists came to their themes in a modern critical spirit, weighing and choosing, deliberating over alternative modes of treatment, bent on finding the right arrangement and proportion. Chaucer's procedure in his adaptations from Boccaccio shows this clearly. *Troilus and Criseyde*, with all its copious detail and all its freedom, is, from one point of view, to put it at its lowest terms, an exercise in composition, a lesson of the workshop. Every page of it, if compared with the Italian original, proves the fine critical sense of Chaucer ; there is no better example in English, if there is any in the world, of studious literary art, which at the same time is perfectly fresh and spirited. Chaucer had the entry of Italian schools of poetry which were not open to Gower. Gower's masters were French ; and French literature had not the same faculties as Italian.

But the French poets also were growing out of the Middle Ages. Compared with the Italians, they are no doubt old-fashioned. They never learned the skill of arrangement, of *ordonnance*, of poetical logic, which came naturally to Boccaccio, and was learned from him, and improved, by Chaucer. They are desultory and diffuse ; and they also keep, unlike the Italians, the simple medieval phrasing, the innocent, garrulous language, which makes Old French sound like the conversation of the Golden Age. At the same time, fourteenth-century French, while in many respects retaining its primitive and unsophisticated grace, was becoming modern in its ideas. Froissart, in his verse even more than his prose, represents the new "urbanity" of the later Middle Ages, the Horatian interest in contemporary manners, which naturally requires a different kind of literature from the old

I

forms of romance or courtly lyric. Froissart's *Buisson de Jeunesse* and *Espinette Amoureuse* are disguised by their old language and their medieval illustrations ; in reality, great part of them belongs to the same class as the Epistles of Horace.

Chaucer had his favourite French poets before him when he wrote polite verse on modern subjects, and his humorous tone is not a new thing ; he shares it with Froissart and Deschamps, just as there is a common manner of speaking and thinking among French and English poets in the time of Dryden or of Pope. Too much has been made of the conventionality of the French school to which Chaucer and Gower belonged. Chaucer is often represented as escaping from the French conventional tradition— found, for instance, in the *Book of the Duchess*—to an independent, humorous view of life in the *Canterbury Tales*. There is less of a contrast between the *Book of the Duchess* and the *Canterbury Tales* than is sometimes supposed. The *Book of the Duchess* has plenty of life in it ; and much of its freedom, its versatility, its gentle changes of tone between the satirical and the elegiac, might be matched in the French poetry of the day. Chaucer got more from the French than their stock devices, such as the allegorical dream and the May morning pageant. And here Gower is Chaucer's ally, his equal, wherever it is possible to compare them, in the polite simplicity,

the perfect ease of conversation, which was the
peculiar gift of the French poets. It is not purely
literary, but depends on an understanding between
the poet and his readers,—a social sympathy, as
M. Gaston Paris has explained so admirably in his
essay on the general character of French literature.[1]
Gower and Chaucer, unlike as they are in genius,
have more of this than most English writers ; Gower
has little else to distinguish him besides this indefinable grace of manner and the elegance of verse which
goes along with it.

Gower's versification has been studied by his editor,
and deserves the care he has bestowed on it. *In tenui
labor* ; it is thin enough, in one sense, but thin like
the music of the clavichord. Gower's art of poetry
is as thorough as if he were using the louder instruments. Fluent as his verse is, there is no " fatal
facility " ; the cadences are tested, the syllables chosen.
An example to which Mr. Macaulay calls attention is
in the vision of ladies in the story of Rosiphelee
(*Conf. Amant.* iv. 1315 *sq.*) :

> In kertles and in copes riche
> Thei weren clothed, alle liche,
> Departed evene of whyt and blew ;
> With alle lustes that sche knew
> Thei were enbrouded overal.
> Here bodies weren long and smal,

---

[1] In the Preface (1896) to the *Histoire de la Langue et de la Littérature
française,* edited by Petit de Julleville.

The beaute faye upon her face
Non erthly thing it may desface ;
Corones on here hed thei beere,
As ech of hem a qweene weere,
That al the gold of Cresus halle
The leste coronal of alle
Ne mihte have boght after the worth :
Thus come thei ridende forth.

Here it is noted that an earlier version read :

The beaute of hire face schon
Wel bryhtere than the cristall ston.

And it may be added that the change to the new reading—"The beaute faye upon her face" (*i.e.* "The fairy beauty on their faces")—is characteristic of Gower's style, both in the choice of the term, the alliteration, and the harmony of the vowels. It is not easy without long quotations to show how good Gower can be ; one cannot tell the beauty of a stream from looking at a selected inch or two. But the following short passage from a lover's soliloquy will prove that Gower, as a "courtly maker," had little to learn (*Conf. Amant.* iv. 605 *sq.*) :

Whi hast thou drede of so good on,
Whom alle vertu hath begon,
That in hire is no violence
Bot goodlihiede and innocence
Withouten spot of eny blame ?
Ha, nyce herte, fy for schame !

Ha, couard herte of love unlered,
Wherof art thou so sore afered,
That thou thi tunge soffrest frese,
And wolt thi goode wordes lese,
Whan thou hast founde time and space ?

Much of Chaucer's lighter verse, especially in the
House of Fame, is, as Mr. Macaulay points out, less
regular than Gower's. There is some fallacy, perhaps, in the comparison. The *House of Fame* was
not written with the same motives as the *Confessio
Amantis*, though it belongs to the same medieval
world and takes pleasure in the same sort of learning.
The *House of Fame* is not honest. The medieval
pedantry in it is meant ironically ; it is not like
Gower's good faith. Chaucer was amusing himself,
in the *House of Fame*, after the exacting work of his
Troilus. In that poem, Pandarus — who no doubt
represents the Italian ideal of culture — had expressly
forbidden the comfortable, easy - going, medieval
fashion of bundling all sorts of discordant things
together. Chaucer knew what he was about when
he proceeded to disregard the prescriptions of
Pandarus ; and so, when he acknowledges in the
House of Fame that the rhyme is " light and lewd,"
the plain certainty is that he meant it to be so. The
House of Fame is not a specimen of Chaucer's art ;
hardly more so, indeed, than the *Rime of Sir Thopas*.
And still, even when the deliberate artlessness of the
House of Fame is left out of account, when Gower and

Chaucer are matched on equal terms, it may appear
that Gower is the more correct poet within his own
compass.   That there is a larger harmony of composition rather than of phrasing, where Gower does
not come into the field against Chaucer, is sufficiently
obvious.   But in the *Book of the Duchess* Chaucer
may be compared with Gower ; the two poets are
here in the same school, and Chaucer has not yet the
ideas and the ambitions which he got from Italy.
Both writers have rendered from Ovid the tale of
Ceyx and Alcyone ; and Mr. Macaulay thinks that
Chaucer has been less successful in reproducing the
story than Gower.   It may be doubted whether this
is so.   Chaucer's phrasing, even in this early conventional work, is more " quick and forgetive " than
Gower's ; for instance, in the description of the valley
of sleep :

> That stant betwixe roches tweye
> Ther never yet grew corn ne gras,
> Ne tre, ne no thing that ought was,
> Best ne man, ne no wiht elles,
> Save ther were a fewe welles
> Came renning fro the cliffes adoun,
> That made a deedly sleping soun,
> And ronnen doun riht by a cave
> That was under a rokke y-grave
> Amidde the valey, wonder depe.

This passage has one line with the English license in
it, dropping a syllable at the beginning—

> Best ne man, ne no wiht elles—

according to the tradition which is found more fully developed in the short verse of Fletcher's *Faithful Shepherdess*, and after that in *L'Allegro*. It is one mark of the difference between Chaucer and Gower ; Gower is more precise, and does not like this variation from the French standard. His description is more detailed, and it has no such beauties as the " deedly sleping soun " of Chaucer's wells ; yet it is good writing :

> And forto speke of that withoute,
> Ther stant no gret tree nyh aboute
> Wher on ther myhte crowe or pie
> Alihte, forto clepe or crie :
> Ther is no cok to crowe day,
> Ne beste non which noise may
> The hell, bot al aboute round
> Ther is growende upon the ground
> Popi, which berth the sed of slep,
> With othre herbes suche an hep.
> A stille water for the nones
> Rennende upon the smale stones,
> Which hihte of Lethes the rivere,
> Under that hell in such manere
> Ther is, which yifth gret appetit
> To slepe.   And thus full of delit
> Slep hath his hous ; and of his couche
> Withinne his chambre if I schal touche,
> Of hebenus that slepi tree
> The bordes al aboute be,
> And for he scholde slepe softe,
> Upon a fethrebed alofte
> He lith with many a pilwe of doun.

It seems no injustice to Gower to say that this is

less good than Chaucer. But in a way it is more correct. Chaucer's irregularity of verse is not allowed by Gower; and this is only one proof of the literary conscience which kept watch over all Gower's writing, and is justified by the·continuous, yet subtly varied eloquence of his narrative.

Gower has no approach to the imaginative world of Chaucer's *Troilus*; it is as far beyond him as Shakespeare is. But he has great skill in giving the right shape to a story, on his own scale and with his own light way of treating dramatic problems. His editor has noted many places in which Gower's judgment is found working to better effect than his masters; he does not follow tamely. In some stories he has improved on Ovid; at any rate, a good case can be made out for him. But his stories are always kept to the simplest terms; there is no drama, except the most elementary. Indeed, it is part of the charm of his stories that they are so simple, so well within the author's powers. Naturally, there is no chance in them for the rich workmanship of Chaucer. They do not touch the mind in the same way. But as pure narrative they are generally admirable. Many examples might be quoted; the story of Rosiphelee, already referred to, is well suited for an illustration of Gower's talent, because it is more or less the same story as Dryden's *Theodore and Honoria*, though the cruel beauty in the

Confessio Amantis is less severely punished. Gower will bear comparison both with Dryden and Boccaccio. The skill with which the story is worked out could only be proved by full quotation. What the style is like has been shown in the quotation given above ; and it needs no long consideration to find out that there Gower has succeeded.

His version of Medea and Jason is worth some attention for various reasons. The story is one in which medieval writers had great chances and some- times took them, because the story is romantic, one might say medieval, from the beginning. Nothing is better fitted for romance than the plot of the king's daughter helping the adventurer with her magic.[1] Gower has gone for his incidents to the first medieval author who told the story as a romance of chivalry, Benoit de Sainte-More, in the *Roman de Troie.* It cannot be said that he has surpassed the French poet, for the author of the *Roman de Troie* was as elegant a poet as Gower, and much stronger in explaining motives ; also, he worked on a larger scale. But it is pleasant to see how Gower acknow- ledges the lasting authority of the early French romantic school by going to the poet of the twelfth century rather than to their common authority, Ovid, for advice ; and how well he keeps the clear, simple lines of the story untroubled by details. As Mr.

[1] Cf. A. Lang, " A Far-travelled Tale," in *Custom and Myth.*

Macaulay shows, Gower revised the incidents so as to keep the most effective parts of the story. He leaves out the earlier tale of Jason (the malignant policy of his uncle sending him on a deadly adventure), because he was not writing a long story, and this part of the plot was not necessary. He passes lightly over the voyage of the Argonauts, and selects the two important things—first, the love of Medea and Jason, with her help in the winning of the Fleece, and secondly, the treachery of Jason, and Medea's revenge. He does not rely for his story on the dull and pretentious Latin of Guido delle Colonne, like Chaucer and the author of the alliterative *Troy Book*. It was a right instinct that led him to the old French.

Gower has, indeed, almost as much in common with twelfth-century French as with Froissart. Although he is in many ways modern in style, in his matter it is otherwise. He is easily contented with what has been long established ; neither his stories nor his moralisings are different in kind from what had been current in France two hundred years before ; and his persevering zeal for classification, however admirable to a medieval taste, would at no time have been applauded for any novelty of spirit or principle. Not that he is remarkably old-fashioned, for along with new ambitions in France at this time there was a rather dismal reproduction of old wares,

an increasing trade in commonplaces, as the works of
Alain Chartier and Christine de Pisan show.

The parts of the *Confessio Amantis* that are
not story-telling have generally been thought the
most monotonous, on account of the formalism of
the Confessor's teaching, and his prosaic division
of the subject under heads like a text-book.   Mr.
Macaulay has done justice to this portion of Gower's
work.   The Lover's account of himself is no mere
repetition of old literary formulas ; and the lady
is not the abstract divinity of the old lyric convention :

> And if hir list to riden oute
> On pelrinage or other stede,
> I come, thogh I be noght bede
> And take hire in min arm alofte
> And sette hire in hire sadel softe,
> And so forth lede hire be the bridel,
> For that I wolde noght ben ydel.
> And if hire list to ride in char,
> And thanne I mai therof be war,
> Anon I schape me to ryde
> Riht evene be the chares side ;
> And as I mai, I speke among,
> And otherwhile I singe a song,
> Which Ovide in his bokes made,
> And seide, " O whiche sorwes glade,
> O which wofull prosperite
> Belongeth to the proprete
> Of love, who so wole him serve !
> And yit therfro mai noman swerve,
> That he ne mot his lawe obeie."
>
> (*Conf. Amant.* iv. 1198, *sq.*)

The 'wofull prosperite' of the last sentence is from the traditional rhetoric ; all the poets were fond of this figure, and it is still in use long after Gower. But what goes before (and there is much besides what has been quoted) is freshly studied, and with some humour. The editor has not neglected the satirical strain in Gower, which is better and more Chaucerian in the *Confessio Amantis* than in the forced invectives of the Latin poem. Mr. Macaulay has noted among other passages one which Chaucer might have written ; it goes to confirm what has been said already, that the ironical quality which is most associated with Chaucer's name is largely a property of the age, as it is also in the days of Steele and Addison. Gower as a moralist takes note of a gentleman's amatory digressions, and touches off his genial conversation with his wife when he comes home again. The pastoral motive, naturally, is not introduced by the husband :

> Bot therof wot nothing the wif
> At hom, which loveth as hir lif
> Hir lord, and sitt alday wisshinge
> After hir lordes hom comynge :
> Bot whan that he comth hom at eve,
> Anon he makth his wif beleve,
> For sche noght elles scholde knowe :
> He telth hire hou his hunte hath blowe,
> And hou his houndes have wel runne,
> And hou ther schon a merye sunne,
> And hou his haukes flowen wel ;
> But he wol telle her nevere a diel

Hou he to love untrewe was,
Of that he robbede in the pas,
And tok his lust under the schawe
Ayein love and ayein his lawe.

(Conf. Amant. v. 6123, sq.)

Even in graver passages Gower shows that the moralist need not fall into prose. The dialogue between the Confessor and the Lover about chivalrous adventures beyond sea, and their value, is not one-sided, but a fair debate between two different standards of virtue. Gower was sceptical regarding the expeditions that young gentlemen made (Henry of Lancaster among them) "their bodies to advance," as Froissart puts it. He does not approve of these "hastyf rodes":

Sometime in Prus, sometime in Rodes,
And sometime into Tartarie.

Especially he refuses to believe that they ought to give advantage in love:

What scholde I winne over the se,
If I mi ladi loste at hom?

The same matter had been discussed in the *Mirour de l'Omme*, and there also with some spirit.

Gower makes little use of heroic verse—the ten-syllable line; but his stanzas in Book VIII. of the *Confessio Amantis*, and the poem addressed to Henry IV. in "rhyme-royal," show that he followed the same laws as Chaucer, particularly in his neglect of the French and Provençal rule—the obligatory pause after the fourth syllable. This is observed by other writers at different times, *e.g.* by the Scottish minstrel, Blind Harry, in his *Wallace* ; in the sixteenth century some theorists upheld it, as Puttenham in the *Arte of English Poesie* (1589) :

The meeter of ten sillables is very stately and heroicall, and must have his *Cesure* fall upon the fourth sillable, and leave sixe behinde him thus :

"I serve at ease, and governe all with woe."

Chaucer does not recognise this as binding, nor do the Italians. This agreement in practice between the English and the Italian poets is not due to borrowing, but to natural affinity. Gower apparently knew no Italian, and his usage is the same as Chaucer's. Even in his French decasyllabic verse in the *Balades* he admits many lines that are incorrect as French verse and right according to the Chaucerian principle ; for example :

La tresplus belle q'unqes fuist humeine,

which has the common English cesura after the fifth syllable, and is consequently irregular. The fact that Gower, with all his strong French sympathies, his careful art, and his fondness for precision, should not have enforced the strict law in English is to the credit of his judgment. Along with Chaucer, he is the founder of heroic verse in English, with the laws and the licenses that are equally familiar to Shakespeare, Milton, Pope, and Tennyson :

> My lord, in whom hath evere yit be founde
> Pite withoute spot of violence,
> Kep thilke pes alwei withinne bounde,
> Which god hath planted in thi conscience :
> So schal the cronique of thi pacience
> Among the seintz be take into memoire
> To the loenge of perdurable gloire.

This, like Gower's octosyllabics, is modern English verse, for the character of the measure is not affected by the antique words and grammar. It is as correct as Pope. Gower's rhyme-royal is not inferior to Chaucer's in any formal respect. It is not only careful : it has the Chaucerian freedom and variety :

> Upon miself is thilke tale come,
> Hou whilom Pan, which is the god of kinde,
> With love wrastlede and was overcome :
> For evere I wrastle and evere I am behinde,
> That I no strengthe in al min herte finde,
> Wherof that I mai stonden eny throwe ;
> So fer mi wit with love is overthrowe.

The agreement between Chaucer and Gower as to the rules of heroic verse makes it all the more difficult to understand the failure of this measure after Lydgate's day, the persistent want of sense among the Chaucerians (except in Scotland) for the chief rhythms of their master, and the extraordinary labour Wyatt had to go through before he made out, if he ever thoroughly made out, what the decasyllabic line was meant for. It is not as if Chaucer had been a lonely and unappreciated artist. In some things, indeed, he was far beyond the range of his time ; but in this he had a companion ; and the heroic verse, so far as the mere mechanism is concerned, was as well understood by Gower as by himself. This, like everything else in the evidence, shows how momentous for literary development the last years of the four-teenth century were, and how utterly their lesson was thrown away in the fifteenth. What the fif-teenth century wanted was not only a genius like Chaucer's, but men of taste like Gower, who might have carried on the forms of poetry for the benefit of more productive ages. As it turned out, Wyatt and Surrey, the refiners of English verse, had to begin at the beginning again—not where Chaucer and Gower left off, but far back among the beggarly elements.

It may be observed, by the way, that decasyllabic verse of what one may call the English type seems to come naturally in the Teutonic languages, when they are imitating the Romance measures. The earliest High German line of this sort, two hundred years before Chaucer, is nearer to Chaucer, or Goethe, than to the Provençal models which Hêr Friderich von Hûsen had before him when he wrote :

O wê wie sol ez armen dir ergân !
Wie torstest eine an solhe nôt ernenden ?
Wer sol dir dîne sorge helfen enden
Mit solhen trouwen als ich hân getân ?

Curiously enough, Froissart is not accurate through-out as the French reckon accuracy ; he writes :

> Comme le papillon à la chandelle,

and

> La premerainne roe qui y loge,—

verses which would have been accepted by Gower, but do not keep the strict rules of the game.

The platitude of Gower's French and Latin works has little to relieve it. The *Mirour de l'Omme*, though it has some merits of style, moving freely enough in a difficult stanza, is far below the *Confessio Amantis*. The Latin elegiacs of the *Vox Clamantis* are generally detestable verse, dressed up in tags from Ovid and other poets, which Mr. Macaulay has carefully marked and referred to their proper authors. The substance of the *Vox Clamantis* has some value, chiefly in the account of Wat Tyler's rebellion, with which it begins. No Latin verses of Gower are better than those which are oftenest quoted from this part :—

> *Grigge* rapit dum *Dawe* strepit comes est quibus *Hobbe*,
>   *Lorkyn* et in medio non minor esse putat,
> *Hudde* ferit quos *Judde* terit dum *Tebbe* minatur,
>   *Jakke* domos que viros vellit et ense necat, etc.

The rest of the book settles down to a thorough

K

criticism of life, with the common medieval pleasure in discovering corruption. Like other work of the sort, it is a source of historical information about manners. The *Cronica Tripertita*, three books of leonine hexameters on the reign of Richard II., or rather on two separate portions of it, is naturally of historical value ; and the editor's commentary here has made it ready for use. But the Latin works altogether add nothing to Gower's literary reputation, except that they show, like the English and French poems, a talent for remembering words. Gower is as copious in Latin as in his other languages, but his finer skill of expression fails him.

The French *Balades* stand by themselves as almost the only work of Gower's not meant to be large and comprehensive, though even here his love of system is active, and he makes them look as dignified as he can. The *balade* in those days was the favourite form for any theme that could be made to fit into it ; Eustache Deschamps and Froissart had written a great number, and new authors were to follow with more. Chaucer in English had perhaps done as much as any of them, with a very few experiments ; at least two of his *balades*—*Absolon* and *Rosemounde*—are among the best pieces in his poetry. Gower did not follow Chaucer here ; his *Cinkante Balades*, dedicated to Henry IV., are in French. They were written when he was an old man, and might pass well enough

for the poetical works of Tithonus, with their impersonal amatory sentiment, their pallid rhetoric, if
only one did not know what a strange demand there
still was for the abstract art of love. Gower makes
one more concession to "the tune of the time" in
these poems, and they add another block of the
polished commonplace to his literary monument.
Still, there is a flutter of life in them; and it is
pleasant to find the old favourite toys again doing
service, the phœnix of Araby, the chameleon living
on air, and so on, with the old tricks of phrase
("wofull prosperite" again) :—

> Pour vous, ma dame, en peine m'esbanoie,
> Jeo ris en plour et en santé languis,
> Jeue en tristour et en seurté m'esfroie,
> Ars en gelée et en chalour fremis.

Indeed, when one remembers that these same things
pleased the Elizabethans, that Euphues made his
fortune out of the same old natural history as provided the similes of Gower, it really becomes difficult
to affirm that the *Balades* are so conventional after
all. No one has ever yet explained the enduring
vogue of all the stock ideas of court poetry; and
Gower's commonplaces are found still current after
many revolutions of taste. Sometimes he has something better, as when he takes up again the story
of Alcyone :—

> Pour remembrer jadis celle aventure
> De Alceone et Ceïx ensement,

Com dieus muoit en oisel lour figure,
Ma volenté serroit tout tielement,
Qe sanz envie et danger de la gent
Nous porroions ensemble par loisir
Voler tout francs en nostre esbatement :
U li coers est, le corps falt obeïr.

Which is not unlike the motive of Dante's sonnet to Guido Cavalcanti :—

Upon a barque with all the winds that blow
Across all seas at our good will to hie.

Besides the *Cinkante Balades* there is another series on loyalty in marriage, which deals more largely in historical examples, as was common with the French school. Many of Gower's are repeated from the *Confessio Amantis*—Jason and Medea, Mundus and Paulina, Alboin and Rosamund. But in nothing except the use of historical names do they come near to Chaucer's *balade* in the *Legend of Good Women*:

Hyd, Absolon, thy gilte tresses clere ;

nor to Froissart in the same poetical form.

Mr. Macaulay's life of Gower, in his fourth volume, is one of his many pieces of careful investigation and criticism. The results, as he says, are chiefly negative, clearing away some traditional errors and some too hasty inferences. John Gower, Esquire, was a friend of Chaucer, and received a power of attorney from him in 1378, to be used during Chaucer's absence abroad ; in 1382 the manors of Feltwell in Norfolk and Multon in Suffolk were granted to him. About the same time, along with "the philosophical Strode," he received the dedication of Chaucer's *Troilus*; in 1393 "Henry of Lancaster presented John Gower, Esquire, with a collar"; in 1398 Gower married Agnes Groundolf; his will was proved in October 1408; and he is buried in St. Saviour's Church. These are almost the only facts discovered, apart from what may be got from his writings. The *Speculum Meditantis* is assigned by Mr. Macaulay to the years 1376-79; the *Confessio Amantis* was certainly complete in 1390, and revised with some alterations by 1393; the *Vox Clamantis* was begun not long after the rebellion of 1381; the *Cronica Tripertita* (like the *Cinkante Balades*) is dated by its dedication to Henry IV., as well as by the matter of the history.

Mr. Macaulay's work may be praised without reserve, except as to small points which do not matter. He has not spared himself. Much of his time must have been taken up with things of small apparent interest; his author's wisdom must have been sometimes more than sufficient during the process of editing and commenting. That the work was worth doing cannot be questioned. Gower, with all his commonplaces, is not like any other writer; and his English poem is still fresh, its simple colours unfaded. Probably it will not be much read: there

are other things to read ; and the public which is
content not to know Crabbe's stories is hardly likely
to take up the *Confessio Amantis*.   But in leisurely
bookish places Gower may recover some of the
attention he used to get from the lovers of poetry.

One fact about his reputation is worth particular
mention.   The *Confessio Amantis* was translated into
Portuguese by Robert Payn, Canon of Lisbon,
apparently in Gower's lifetime ; his work survives in
a Castilian version, to which Mr. Macaulay's attention
was called by Mr. Fitzmaurice Kelly, and from which
he gives two quotations, one from the preface—" for
king Richardes sake "—the other the greeting to
Chaucer.   The Portuguese was probably, like the
Castilian version, in prose.   It is a pleasant literary
memorial of the old alliance and sympathy between
England and Portugal—perhaps one good result of
the Duke of Lancaster's expedition to the Peninsula.
Gower, we would say, was well selected for translation.
Spanish literature in the fifteenth century, for all its
Italian studies, was not far advanced beyond the
learning of Gower ; the Marquis of Santillana, for
example, moves in almost the same order of ideas
and subjects.

FROISSART

THE *Chronicles* of Froissart is among the books
which have received the fullest share of honour of all
kinds, from their own day to the present, without
any grudging voice being raised against their triumph,
or any sensible diminution of their renown. Froissart is still the name that stands for chivalrous
adventure in the minds of all readers of history ; he
is accepted without question as the author from
whom the portraiture of that age is to be sought.
The signs of his fame are everywhere : in the great
libraries, in glorious manuscripts like the Harleian
one, in the old printed copy that Lord Hunsdon
used as a family Bible to record on its fly-leaf the
births of his children, in a thousand testimonies
from writers of all sorts, among which chiefly those
of Gray and of Scott are memorable. Gray called
him " the Herodotus of a barbarous age," and recommended him to his correspondents. Scott, whose
French visitors found that he talked the language of
the old chronicles when he was at a loss for modern

words in speaking to them, has put the praise of Froissart in the mouth of Claverhouse, and has expressed it in this indirect way, in *Old Mortality*, more vividly than in a review or an historical essay. Lord Berners was happily led in his undertaking to translate the *Chronicles*, though indeed one may believe that with his tastes it was hardly possible for him to do otherwise. This book of Lord Berners is one that put the English tongue in possession of something on which the whole Western world, for generations past, had relied for information about itself and its manners. That Froissart should be turned into English before the last reflection of the age of Froissart had died away in the new era of the sixteenth century, that the courtly poet and historian of the times of Edward III. should be brought by translation into a closer partnership with Chaucer, was a thing to be desired more than most of the literary things provided under the reign of Henry VIII. ; and it was fortunately accomplished by the man whose mission it might seem to have been to rescue as much as he could of the treasures of the Middle Ages before they were overwhelmed by new learning. He translated Froissart, he translated *Huon of Bordeaux*.

I

Lord Berners is a follower of Chaucer and Malory as an interpreter in English of some of the courtly French literature which was for the most part so imperfectly understood, though so generously admired, in the island of Britain. What the English had been deprived of by the accidents of their history was the peculiar glory of the Middle Ages ; they had no proper courtly romance, no chivalrous stories in their own language of the same temper as those of France. Many things are attainable in a literature like that of England between the Norman Conquest and the Revival of Learning ; but what was not attainable before Chaucer, and very feebly remembered after him, was precisely that sort of grace which belongs to a Court, to a refined affected mode of sentiment, like that of the *Romaunt of the Rose.* Before Chaucer and Gower acquired it, the English had not the right of entry to that world ; and in most of their persevering studies of the way to be gentle, they are little better than the ambitious gallants in Elizabethan comedy whose education has been neglected, the Gullios who learn manners by the book of compliments. Nothing in history is more desperate than the attempts of English writers under the Plantagenets to master the secret of French courtliness. Sometimes the failure is ludicrous, as in the

" rime doggerel " of the ordinary minstrels ; sometimes there is success of another sort, as in the great alliterative poems, which are not courtly in the French manner, though they are magnificent. Meantime, the days go by and the fashion changes, and but for Chaucer and a few others there might have been nothing left in English with the character most distinctive of those times—the singular quality of beauty found in the medieval literature of France. Later, when the medieval forms were still nearer their vanishing, at the hour " when all the lights grow dim," the most notable work of French romance, in which all the graces, and not those of the Courts only, are included, the stories of Lancelot, Tristram, the Quest of the Grail and the *Mort Artus*, were rendered by Sir Thomas Malory in language that remains among the most wonderful things of the world. The reproach of England was taken away, though late and with difficulty. Nothing could give to England of the time of Henry III. such poems and stories as were written in other lands in those days ; but under Edward IV. it was not yet impossible to recover from the past, out of " the French book," a version of the stories that had been too high for the landward-bred and simple-minded English authors to copy fairly, in the bygone times when " the French book " was still new. What happened with Froissart was something of the same

kind. There was not enough of the fourteenth
century represented in English literature. Even
after all that Chaucer had done, there was something
left to do. Chaucer had gone beyond his age in
many respects ; he is greater than Froissart ; but in
the same measure that he surpasses him in imagination
and in art he leaves room for the other man with his
other mode of regarding and rendering the world.
Froissart's mode is more peculiarly and thoroughly
the property of the fourteenth century than
Chaucer's, through his very want of those affinities
with Shakespeare and Cervantes that are found in
the variety of Chaucer's workmanship and in his
more liberal genius. Just as England, so long im-
peded and depressed by the historical accidents of its
language, obtained from Malory some of the riches
of the thirteenth century, which at the time when
they were first produced it had no skill to make its
own, so from Lord Berners it received back Froissart, not too late to make amends for the loss it had
suffered through the want of such a chronicler in the
native tongue. It was by an injustice of fortune
that England had been refused in the Middle Ages
an historian writing English as other tongues were
written by the French, Italian, and Spanish authors,
by Villehardouin, Joinville, Froissart, by Villani, by
Ayala, by Ramon Muntaner, by the Provençal
biographers of the poets. What could be done to

redress this grievance was done by Lord Berners for
history, as by Malory for romance ; and the fourteenth century, illustrious in the English language
by so many things of a different kind, by *Troilus*
and the *Canterbury Tales*, by the poems of *Sir
Gawain* and of *Piers Plowman*, to name no more,
was now presented with a new author, who belonged
even more closely and intimately to the reign of
Edward III. than Chaucer himself : an author whose
whole business, it might be said, was to live in the
fourteenth century and tell what he saw there.

Lord Berners is not among the greatest of translators—his rank is nearer Caxton than Malory—but
his version of Froissart is a true version : it is really
Froissart in English, and in English that sounds like
Froissart.   As Malory gives in English (with much
of his own besides) the tone of the old French
language of the *Queste del St. Graal*, so the sentences
of Lord Berners' translation are of the fourteenth
century and not of the sixteenth.   He tried
occasionally to write a style of his own, and
was proud of it, no doubt : it appears in his
prefaces,— a style rhetorical and cultivated.   He
also translated, besides these *Chronicles* and the
stories of *Sir Huon* and *Arthur of Little Britain*,
two modern works, one of which, the *Golden Book of
Marcus Aurelius*, written in Spanish by Guevara, has
a reputation as the parent of *Euphues*, while the

other, also Spanish, of an earlier generation, the
Prison of Love, by Diego de San Pedro, has the
same Euphuistic syntax, and probably did a great
deal to establish the new fashion of prose that was
taken up long afterwards by Lyly and his contemporaries.   Two opposite kinds of prose are represented in the works translated by Lord Berners.   On
the one hand are the writers who write because they
have something to say, whether it be the story of the
wars of England, France, Scotland, and Spain, or the
wanderings of Sir Huon in Fairyland.   On the other
are the Spanish Euphuists explaining, to a world that
runs its clauses into one another, endlessly, the
counter doctrine of precise constructions and elegant
phrases.   Rhetoric flourished under the Tudors,
along with religious controversy, in the silence of
the poets ; it put many honest people out of conceit
with their old-fashioned romances.   Lord Berners
does not allow it to vitiate his Froissart.   His
Euphuist translations came later than his Froissart
for one thing, and he does not seem to have had any
particular affection for that variety of prose, though
his preface to Froissart shows that other kinds of
rhetorical display had an occasional attraction for him.
Such things are kept out of his translation of the
history : the body of his Froissart bears hardly a
trace of the rhetoric that illuminates the Prologue.
The good taste of Lord Berners, which is not con-

spicuous in his few original paragraphs, is shown in his devotion to his author, and in his refusal to let the original style be misrepresented. His very want of literary ambition saves him : he trusts in the matter of the story, and the right words find themselves translating the right words of the French. It is not always the case that a writer is saved by his subject : there are many historians, from Ammianus Marcellinus to Saxo Grammaticus, who have told good stories in extravagant words, with a dictionary broken loose and rampant over their pages. But it happens sometimes that the matter prescribes the form, and this was the case with Lord Berners, as it may have been with Froissart himself. The history has no grammar or forms of sentence that in any way interrupt the narrative. It is in the old style— the style of the French medieval historian. The fourteenth century is not defrauded in this translation by the imposition of any Tudor order of rhetoric on the clear outlines of the structure. It is with Lord Berners as with King James's translators of the Bible : in the Preface they indulge themselves, but their main work is different and contains nothing the least resembling " that bright occidental star " which shines in the Dedication to the King.

II

Sir John Bourchier,[1] second Lord Berners, was born about 1467, and succeeded his grandfather, the first Baron, in 1474. "A martial man, well seen in all military discipline," is the phrase in which Fuller describes him among the Worthies of Hertfordshire ; and the record of his life, which is not full, is that of a loyal servant of the king. He took part in the discomfiture of the Cornish rebels at Blackheath in 1496 and in other warfare later, as at the capture of Terouenne in 1513. He went in an embassy to Spain in 1518, and suffered from want of money through the winter that followed ; he borrowed afterwards from King Henry VIII., and left the king his creditor at the end of his life. His career is a good deal like that of Sir Thomas Wyatt, with less adventure in it, and nothing comparable to Wyatt's heroic encounter with the Emperor Charles, but showing the same devotion to the service in which he was engaged.

In December 1520 Lord Berners was made deputy of Calais, and held the office till his death in March

[1] The life of Lord Berners has been written by Mr. Sidney Lee in his Introduction to the *Boke of Duke Huon of Burdeux* (Early English Text Society, 1882-1887) and in the *Dictionary of National Biography*, and by Mr. G. C. Macaulay in his Introduction to *Berners' Froissart* in the Globe Edition.

1533. It was at Calais, probably, that all his writing was done, and his writing for those years must have been a chief part of his occupation. The public interest was not neglected by him, but one may judge from the bulk of his writings—the *Chronicles of Froissart*, *Huon of Bordeaux*, *Arthur of Little Britain* —how large an amount of time must have been spent at the desk in matters not belonging to the office of governor. The *Chronicles* of Froissart was published in 1523 and 1525—two volumes, "imprinted at London in Fletestrete by Richarde Pynson, printer to the kinges moost noble grace." From this work Lord Berners went on to his translation of romances. It is not known whether or not the *Boke of Duke Huon of Burdeux* was published in his lifetime — that is, before March of 1533. The earliest extant copy of *Huon of Burdeux*, according to Mr. Lee's judgment in his edition of the romance, was printed about 1534, probably by Wynkyn de Worde. *The hystory of the moost noble and valyaunt knyght Arthur of lytell brytayne, translated out of frensshe in to englushe by the noble Johan Bourghcher knyght lorde Barners* was printed by Robert Redborne, without date. Whatever the order in which these works were translated, they probably came after Froissart and before the smaller books taken (indirectly) from the Spanish : the *Castell of Love* and the *Golden Boke of Marcus*

Aurelius Emperour and eloquent oratour. The colophon of the latter gives its date of composition ; in the uncertainty of Lord Berners' literary history the dates of Froissart and of the *Golden Book* are fairly well determined :—" Thus endeth the volume of Marke Aurelie emperour, otherwise called the golden boke, translated out of Frenche into englyshe by John Bourchier knyghte lorde Barners, deputie generall of the kynges toune of Caleis and marches of the same, at the instant desire of his neuewe syr Francis Bryan knyghte, ended at Caleys the tenth day of Marche in the yere of the Reygne of our souerayn lorde kynge HENRY the viii. the XXIII." So in the edition of 1536 and most others ; the first edition of 1534 is said to read xxiiii. The twenty-third year of King Henry is 1532, the twenty-fourth is 1533; and according to this the *Golden Book* was finished by Lord Berners six days before his death, for he died on the 16th of March in 1533, and the book was finished on the 10th.

It is probably vain to suppose that the transition from romance to courtly rhetoric, shown in the selection of Guevara after *Huon of Bordeaux*, is significant of any progress or change of taste in the translator. Lord Berners, with all his literary skill, is careless about distinctions of kinds : he is not critical nor scrupulous. His choice of the *Golden*

L

Book does not mean that he was tired of history or romance ; it does not mean that he had been convinced of the laxity of old-fashioned syntax, and was bent on living cleanly according to the rules of the point-device grammarians. It means only that the *Golden Book* was in favour, as *Huon* had been and continued to be, and that Lord Berners, with his love of stories undiminished, was yet willing to take up another kind of book in which gentlefolk found pleasure and entertainment. That Lord Berners is not to be trusted for critical appreciation is shown in his attention to *Arthur of Little Britain.* For the story of *Huon of Bordeaux*, at least for the earlier part, there is nearly as much to be said as for the adventures of the *Morte D'Arthur* itself, considered as a specimen of authentic romance, such as was current in the best ages, and was fitted to be read by the author of the *Faery Queene.* But *Arthur of Little Britain* is a different story, not among the best, but one of the mechanical rearrangements of the common matter that repeated the old stock incidents and sentiments wearily,—a book that one would save, indeed, from the judgment of the curate and the barber, but more for the honour of its ancestry and for the noble language, than for any merit in the author's imagination. The translation may be reckoned among the fine achievements of Lord Berners : its style is that of his

Froissart, and is enough to make one repent of having spoken harshly about the story of the *Petit Artus de Bretaigne*. The preface of the translator reveals the mind of Lord Berners more clearly than anything else in the scanty sum of his personal utterances. He is not an acute, discreet rhetorician : he is immersed in the matter of old chronicles so that he cannot tell the waking from the dreaming vision ; so much absorbed in the charm of narrative that any narrative has power to draw him. He plunges into the story of *Arthur of Little Britain* before he knows where he is or what it is about ; only when he has gone some way there comes a shock of misgiving, and he repents that he has engaged upon " a fayned mater wherin semeth to be so many unpossybylytees." However, he is in it and may as well go on ; *urceus exit* ; if it will not do for a sober chronicle, it is a story, at any rate ; and there are others, much respected, in which there are equally wonderful things. But the whole Preface must be quoted, and it hardly needs a commentary to explain what was in the mind of Lord Berners when he wrote it ; his good faith, his perfectly sincere delight in narrative, his secondary regard, by an afterthought, for the author's " vertuous entent " ; his admiration, without the heat of a competitor, for proficiency in " fresh ornate polished English " and the " facundious art of rhetoric."

Here foloweth the Translatour's Prologue : For as moche as it is delectable to all humayne nature to rede and to here these auncient noble hystoryes of the chyvalrous feates and marciall prowesses of the vyctoryous knyghtes of tymes paste, whose tryumphaunt dedes, yf wrytynge were not, sholde be had clene oute of remembraunce ; and also bycause that ydelnesse is reputed to be the moder of al vices ; wherfore somwhat in eschewynge therof, and in the waye of lowli erudycyon and learnynge, I John Bourghchere knyghte lorde Berners have enterprysed to translate out of Frensshe in to our maternall tongue a noble hystory, makynge mencyon of the famous dedes of the ryght valyaunt knyght Arthur sonne and heyre to the noble duke of Brytayne, and of the fayre lady Florence, doughter and heyre to the myghty Emendus, kynge of the noble realme of Soroloys, and of the grete trouble that they endured, or they attayned to the perfourmance of theyr vertuous amorous desyers ; for fyrste they overcame many harde and straunge adventures, the whiche as to our humayne reason sholde seme to be incredible. Wherfore after that I had begon this sayd processe I had determined to have left and gyven up my laboure, for I thoughte it sholde have ben reputed but a folye in me to translate be seming suche a fayned mater, wherin semeth to be so many unpossybylytees. How be it than I called agayne to my remembraunce that I had redde and seen many a sondrye volume of dyverse noble hystoryes wherin were contayned the redoubted dedes of the auncyent invynsyble conquerours and of other ryght famous knyghtes who acheved many a straunge and wonderfull adventure, the whyche by playne letter as to our understandynge sholde seme in a maner to be supernaturall : wherfore I thought that this presennt treatyse myght as well be reputed for trouth as some of those, and also I doubted not but that the first auctour of this boke devysed it not with out some maner of trouthe or vertuous entent. The whyche consyderacyons, and other, gave me agayne audacyte to contynue forth my fyrste purpose tyll I had fynysshed this sayd boke, not presumynge that I have reduced it in to fresshe ornate polysshed Englysshe, for I know myself insufficient in the facondyous arte of rethoryke, nor also I am but a lerner of the language of Frensshe.   How be it, I truste my symple reason hath ledde to the understandynge of the true sentence of the mater, accordinge to the whiche I have folowed as nere as I coude, desyrynge all the reders and herers therof to take this my rude translacion in gre, and yf any faute be, to laye it to myn unconnynge and derke ingnor-aunce, and to mynysshe, adde or augment as they shall fynde cause requysyte.   And in theyr so doynge I shall praye to God that after this vayne and transytory lyfe he may brynge them unto the perdurable joye of heven.   *Amen.*

Thus endeth the Translatour's Prologue.

Lord Berners is a fortunate writer, whatever mistakes he may have made about *Arthur of Little Britain*.   He was not turned aside by vanities : "the facundious art of rhetoric" did not corrupt him beyond a few innocent traces of ornamental language in his preliminary discourses.   It was not his genius to do "any eclipsing thing," like *Euphues* ; while he had the instinct for sound language in con-tinuous narration, of the kind that does not glare or flash, and may easily escape notice for its goodness till some occasion comes to test it.   How well the ordinary sentences of Berners will come through examination has been shown by Sir Henry Craik in his comparison of Berners' *Froissart* with Johnes's.[1]

[1] *English Prose Selections,* i. 123 *sq.*

The excellence of Lord Berners is nothing dazzling or astounding ; it comes from a secure command of the right words, in plenty sufficient for all his purposes, with an easy syntax, easily corresponding to his French originals, and turning them into English without any grammatical heaviness or sign of labour. As compared to Malory there is a want of volume and variety in Lord Berners, due no doubt in part to the character of the text he was translating ; for Froissart, with all his glory, is not like Malory's "French book" in opportunities for splendid diction, and Huon's ally, Oberon, is too substantial and sensible a personage for the enchanted twilight of the *Morte D'Arthur*. But, failing the greatest qualities of Malory's prose, there is nothing wanting to Lord Berners in the kind of literature he has chosen. He comes at the end of the Middle Ages in a reign not distinguished by much good writing, when poetry in England is nearly dead, and when prose is threatened by a recurrence of the old ornamental pedantries of "facondyous rethoryke," with the alternative of a rather prim correctness under the rule of classical scholars. His success consists in his steady following of the old fashion, the medieval fashion, of composition, with a regard for just such excellences of form as are convenient in such a mode of writing. Lord Berners used the medieval syntax so as to give few openings for

censure, even from exacting critics ; and before the
confused Elizabethan time, when prose seemed
capable of most things except self-command, he
showed how clearness, simplicity, an even and continuous discourse, might be obtained without depart-
ing ostensibly from the syntax of the fourteenth
century. Any sentences from his *Froissart* will
exhibit this plain, straightforward style in its simplicity and security :—

Thus at the beginnynge the Frenchmen and they of
Aragon fought valiantly, so that the good knightes of
Englande endured moche payne. That day Sir Johan
Chandos was a good knight, and dyde under his baner many
a noble feate of armes ; he adventured himselfe so farre that
he was closed in amonge his enemyes, and so sore overpressed
that he was felled downe to the erthe. And on him there
felle a great and a bigge man of Castell, called Martyne
Ferrant, who was gretly renomed of hardynesse amonge the
Spanyardes, and he dyde his entent to have slayne Sir Johan
Chandos, who lay under him in great danger. Than Sir
Johan Chandos remembered of a knyfe that he had in his
bosome, and drewe it out, and strake this Martyne so in the
backe and in the sydes that he wounded him to dethe as he
lay on him. Than Sir Johan Chandos tourned hym over,
and rose quickely on his fete ; and his men were there aboute
hym, who had with moche payne broken the prease to come
to hym, wher as they saw him felled.

There is nothing remarkable about this sort of
English except that it cannot be bettered. There
is no particular formula for it : only, it shows a care

for rhythm such as was not always found along with the care for classical periods in the writers of that time. The grammar of Lord Berners is one that pays attention to the right spacing of phrases according to their weighty syllables : when this is assured, there is less need for the grammatical complications of clauses in their right order and degree ; the easy constructions of the old style leave it free to the author to tune his syllables to his own mind. The grammatical pattern of the classical schools has little attraction for him when he is taken up with the other device, of free enunciation with no broken, confused, or jarring sounds to break the tenor of it.

There is nothing in Lord Berners like the exorbitant fondness for novel and emphatic words, splendid or swaggering, such as are noted in some of the Elizabethan translators. He has a rich and full vocabulary, but it does not blaze out in single gems. It corresponds to the vocabulary of Froissart, the beauty of which, as of all good French, and not least in the French medieval prose, lies in the harmony between the single words and the syntactic idiom. The prose is not a new invention ; it is natural, in the sense that it is founded upon the usages of conversation, quick and expressive, well provided with plenty of words for interesting things, unimpeded by drawling rhetoric, and free from any anxiety or curiosity about rules of good taste, because it had good taste to begin with, and did not need to think about it. The speech of Aymerigot Marcel, for instance, which may be pondered word for word and phrase for phrase as an infallible piece of good syntax and good diction, is expressed altogether in common and well-established forms, from the beginning, "Ha! a! du traiteur vieillart, dist Aymerigot," to the end, "comment qu'il prende ne adviegne du nouvel." This is rendered not quite fully by Lord Berners, but in the right manner of the original, with the same security and absence of constraint :—

Than tydinges came to Aymergot Marcell, where he was purchasyng of frendes to have reysed the siege before the fortresse of Vandoys, that it was gyven up. Whan he herde therof he demaunded howe it fortuned : it was shewed hym howe it was by reason of a skrymysshe, and by the issuying out of his uncle Guyot du Sall unadvysedly. Ah, that olde traytour, quod Aymergot ; by saynte Marcell, if I had hym here nowe, I shulde sle hym with myne owne handes ; he hath dyshonoured me and all my companyons. At my departynge I straytely enjoyned hym that for no maner of assaute or skrymysshe made by the Frenchmen he shulde in no wyse open the barryers, and he hath done the contrary : this domage is nat to be recovered, nor I wote nat whether to go. They of Caluset and they of Donsac wyll kepe the peace, and my companyons be spredde abrode lyke men dyscomfyted ; they dare never assemble agayne togyther ; and though I had them togyther, yet I wote nat whyder to bring them. Thus, all thynge consydred, I am in a harde parte, for I have gretly dyspleased the French kynge, the duke of Berrey, and the lordes of Auvergne, and all the people of the countrey, for I have made them warre the peace durynge : I had trusted to have won, but I am nowe in a great adventure to lese, nor I wotte nat to whom to resorte to axe counsayle. I wolde nowe that I and my goodes with my wyfe were in Englande ; there I shulde be in surety ; but howe shulde I get thyder and cary all my stufe with me ? I shulde be robbed twenty tymes or I coulde gette to the see, for all the passages in Poictou, in Rochell, in Fraunce, in Normandy and in Pycardy are straytely kept ; it wyll be harde to scape fro takyng : and if I be taken, I shall be sente to the Frenche kynge, and so I shall be loste and all myne. I thynke the surest way for me were to drawe to Burdeaulx, and lytell and lytell to get my good thyder, and to abyde there tyll the warre renewe agayne, for I have good hoope that after this treuce warre shall be open agayne bytwene Englande and Fraunce. Thus Aymergot Marcell debated the matter in hymselfe ; he was hevy and sorowfull, and wyste nat what waye to take, outher to recover some fortresse in Auvergne, or els to go to Burdeaux, and to sende for his wife thider, and for his goodes lytell and lytell secretely. If he hadde done so, he had taken the surest waye ; but he dyde contrary, and therby lost all, lyfe and godes. Thus fortune payeth the people whan she hath sette them on the highest parte of her whele, for sodainly she reverseth them to the lowest parte, ensample by this Aymergotte. It was sayde he was well worthe a hundred thousande frankes, and all was lost on a daye ; wherfore I may well saye that fortune hath played her pagiaunt with hym, as she hath done with many mo, and shall do.

The French is better and more lively, breaking out, for instance, in exclamation after the reference to the truce ("après ces trièves, *mal fuissent elles*

prinses ne venues, entre France et Angleterre ") ;
but the English, though less mercurial, is the
language of one who is free-born, and who has not
had to pay the price of the weary rhetorical schools
for his command of phrases.

There are blemishes, of course, in Lord Berners'
Froissart. There are mistranslations and confusions.
But these hardly affect the reputation of the book as
a history well written and pleasant to read. " It
might have been better, if the author had taken
more pains "—this respectable formula comes to
mind rather too often in the presence of Lord
Berners' easy-going translations, which sometimes
recall the humours of the *Ayenbite of Inwyt*, " mills-
to-the-wind " and such like. But the mistakes are
not enough to spoil the story, any more than the
Psalms have been spoilt in Coverdale's version, and
others, by similar failures.

It is something against the vogue of Lord
Berners—a small thing—that he lived in a time when
English spelling had contrived to make the language
look other than beautiful. It is unfortunate that his
clear phrases should be muffled in the misplaced and
useless spellings that seem exactly the right dress for
the shambling verse of the poets of that day.
" Barkesse " and " marchesse " (for " barks " and
" marches "), " physycyon," " pertaynynge," " cherys-
shynge," " concludedde," and so forth, are well

enough for decrepit Chaucerian allegories, and for such moral interludes as make desolate the Tudor reigns for more than half the century ; but we could have wished Lord Berners a habit better fitted for his mode of narrative, something less cumbrous, like the spelling of Chaucer or of Dunbar. Unhappily to this grievance, if such it be, Lord Berners has added considerably—partly through the fault of his French text, partly through the original and acquired ineptitude of the printer, but with more than can be fairly put down to their discredit—by his unqualified neglect of the historical names. It is beyond all language of complaint. The man who has been led into the intricate fallacies of the names in Berners' *Froissart* is only too glad to escape in silence.

III

The *Castell of Love* and the *Golden Boke of Marcus Aurelius* are different in kind from the other translations of Lord Berners, as well as much less imposing in size. What they want in bulk they make up in pretensions of another sort : it is in these that Lord Berners shows himself a Euphuist, and the *Golden Boke* especially has had ascribed to it by some critics the honour of having first introduced the rhetorical antithetic manner into English. It is impossible to say, in our ignorance about the shadowy character of

Lord Berners, what motives led him to these books, or whether he really saw much good in their contrasted kinds of vanity. The *Castell of Love* is an allegory of the school of the *Romaunt of the Rose* ; the *Golden Boke*, so called by its author, is a pompous exercise in ornamental sentences by a disciple of the new learning. There is no need to think of the *Chronicles* of Froissart in order to show up the tenuity of the one and the inanity of the other ; the history of *Arthur of Little Britain* by comparison to either of them looks almost as substantial and as full of vitality as *Don Quixote*. Of course, as Froissart himself has proved, and Chaucer also, it is possible for a man to love at one and the same time the history of real characters and the phantoms of allegory ; but in the careless versions of the *Carcel de Amor* and the *Libro Aureo* there is no sign of any strong affection for either work. We may be sure that Lord Berners was fond of stories ; it is not proved that he had a liking either for the old courtly manner of allegory or for the new pedantry of moralising. In default of other theories about his literary taste, we may accept the statement of these two books as exactly true : they were done to order, " at the instance of the Lady Elizabeth Carew," who asked for the *Castell of Love*, and " at the instant desire of his nephew Sir Francis Brian, knight," who admired the *Libro Aureo*. Both books were much in favour, and

Lord Berners, whatever may be said against his Euphuistic clients, has the advantage, if that be anything, of having kept his English readers well abreast of contemporary literature in translating them. They were what every one in Italy, Spain, and France was reading, or wishing to read, or ashamed to be supposed not to have read. Most probably he cared very little for them himself.

The two rhetorical books are very much unlike one another except in the common taste for a particular kind of sentence. It is quite possible to fall into the idle mood for which the simple allegory of the *Carcel de Amor* seems occupation enough, and with nothing strained or absurd in its gentle, honourable sentiments. For the sake of the Garden of the Rose, and Chaucer's Anelida, and "the floure of hem that maken in France," and all the great company of the chivalrous poets, it may be granted to this late author of the *Castell of Love* to show the way back over seldom-trodden ground into the old pleasances, the dreamy air, the vanishing courts and temples of the Hollow Land. "Many are the Mighty Ones," and there is still some power in those shadows of old poetry, though few steps wander now into the region of their enchantment. Perhaps now and then a careless bibliographer, when he thinks least of danger, may find himself caught by the spell.

There is no such danger and no such charm in the *Golden Boke*, however much it may have prided itself, and called itself the *Dial of Princes*, and made the Emperor Marcus Aurelius help in the furtherance of its pretentious conceit. The Golden Book so styled is really a Brazen Calf, of the pattern invented specially for the Renaissance and its idolaters. The author, Antonio Guevara, Bishop of Guadix and of Mondoñedo, had a taste for sounding moral sentences, and for criticism of life in the manner of Polonius. He included also in his theory the principles of Iago's moral essay on the *Characters of Women*, which are not those of the *Castell of Love*. Nothing could be more unlike the chivalry of Diego de San Pedro than the brisk remarks about the inferiority of women in the other Euphuist ; both authors seem to have been equally popular, though the points of view are hardly reconcilable, except through the rhetorical taste that the two writers have in common. The casuistry of the amorist San Pedro is expressed in the same manner of writing as " the answere of M. themperour whan Faustyne his wife demaunded the key of his study," a lecture to inquisitive females which is not now so well known as it deserves to be.

That the Spanish authors were the first to give currency to the antithetic way of phrasing adopted by Euphues seems to be proved, and in the history of this kind of prose Diego de San Pedro comes before Guevara. It was of course a very old device, as Plato bears witness ;[1] but it was in Spain at the end of the fifteenth century that it was established as the proper manner of good composition, and the *Carcel de Amor* was one of the books that taught it.[2]

---

[1] The speech of Agathon in the *Symposium* is pure Euphues, and is reported by Plato with the same motive and the same zest as Shakespeare had in his rhetorical parodies in *Love's Labour's Lost* and elsewhere :—
οὗτος δὲ ἡμᾶς ἀλλοτριότητος μὲν κενοῖ, οἰκειότητος δὲ πληροῖ, τὰς τοιάσδε ξυνόδους μετ' ἀλλήλων πάσας τιθεὶς ξυνιέναι, ἐν ἑορταῖς, ἐν χοροῖς, ἐν θυσίαις γιγνόμενος ἡγεμὼν πραότητα μὲν πορίζων, ἀγριότητα δ' ἐξορίζων, φιλόδωρος εὐμενείας, ἄδωρος δυσμενείας, etc., *Symp.* 197 D. Earlier in the same dialogue the fashionable mode is touched upon, "for in this way the learned instruct me to keep the balance of syllables" :—Παυσανίου δὲ παυσαμένου, διδάσκουσι γάρ με ἴσα λέγειν οὑτωσὶ οἱ σοφοί, 185 C.

[2] Composed by Diego de San Pedro, at the request of Diego Hernandez, master of the pages (*alcayde de los donzeles*) and of other gentlemen of the Court. Printed by "The Four Companions" at Seville in 1492, and by "Fadrique aleman de Basilea" (Frederick of Basle) at Burgos in 1496. A Catalan version, Barcelona, Johan Rosenbach, is dated 1493. Diego de San Pedro repented of his very innocent vanity, and wrote a palinode confessing the blindness and errors of the *Carcel de Amor* : reprinted from the *Cancionero General*, Valencia, 1511, by Böhl de Faber, *Floresta de Rimas Antiguas Castellanas*, i. p. 152. The *Carcel de Amor* has alternative conclusions, the second written by Nicolas Nuñez : this addition is found in Berners' *Castell of Love*. Thus England comes into some slight relation with the poets of the court of Castile, who might have given better entertainment than is provided in their treatises and allegories, if Lord Berners had gone to the *Cancionero* instead of to their prose. Nicolas Nuñez has a beautiful poem to Our Lady, written in the measure which was not accepted in England till long after :—

> O Virgen que a Dios pariste
> y nos diste
> a todos tan gran victoria,
> torname alegre de triste
> pues podiste
> tornar nuestra pena en gloria.—*Floresta*, i. p. 7.

A crucial instance to show this may be found in the dedications of different versions of the book. It was translated from Spanish into Italian, from Italian into French, from French into English. The dedications are different in the different languages, but one Euphuistic sentence is common to them all, and in the Italian and the French especially it stands out in contrast with what may be supposed the natural style, or rather the favourite affectations, of the translators :—

"Como quiera que primero que me determinasse estuve en grandes dubdas ; vista vuestra discrecion temia, mirada vuestra virtud osava ; en lo uno hallava el miedo, y en lo otro buscava la seguridad ; y en fin escogí lo mas dañoso para mi verguença, y lo mas provechoso para lo que devia."

Carcel de Amor, 1496.

"E ben che io stessi in gran dubio prima ch' io me determinassi, perche vedendo la sublimità e intellegentia sua io temevo, mirando la prudentia e virtute io havevo ardire ; in l' una trovavo il timore, ne l' altra cercavo la sicurezza ; in fine elessi il più dannoso per la mia vergogna e 'l più utile per il mio debito."

Carcer d' Amore del magnifico Meser Lælio de' Man-fredi. Venice, 1514.

"Pour laquelle chose premier que en ce labeur cultiver me determinasse en grande dubiosité et diversité d'ymagina-tions me trouvay. Car voyant la sublimité et intelligence de ton esperit ie craignoye, et premeditant la prudence et vertu m'enhardissoye et prenoye vigueur tres grande. En l'ung trouvoye la timeur et en l'autre seureté et hardyesse.

M

En fin ie esleuz le plus dommageable pour ma vergogne et le plus utile pour mon devoir."

> *La Prison d'Amours, laquelle traicte de l'amour de Leriano et de Laureole,* faict en Espaignol, puis translaté en tusquan, et nagueres en langage francois.   Paris, 1526.

"For or I first entred into this rude laboure, I was brought into great doubtfulnes, and founde myself in dyvers ymaginacions.   For seyng the quycke intelligence of your spirite I feared, and againe the remembraunce of your vertue and prudence gave me audacite.   In the one I founde feare, and in the other suertie and hardynes.   Fynally, I did chose the moste unvaylable for myne owne shame and most utylitie. . . ."

After this in Lord Berners' text there is some confusion, due either to his habit of abridging, which sometimes interferes with the sense in *Froissart,* or to a printer's error.   It does not matter much.   The striking thing is that this passage of Euphuism is the only thing directly translated from the Spanish prologue in the Italian, and therefore, as the French translator had not the Spanish to work from, the only sentence of San Pedro's represented in the French dedication ; and it is quite different in rhetorical form from the Italian and the French contexts, which again are different from one another. Lelio de' Manfredi of Ferrara uses another kind of ornament altogether, the language of Don Adriano or Sir Piercy Shafton, and not of the authentic Euphues : " flattery and fustian," quite unlike the

neat syntactical play of the Spaniard. The Italian
author, when left to himself, writes as follows :—
"Che havendo con non pocha diligentia e faticha
ridutto questo picciol volume da lo externo idioma
in nostra vernacula lingua a V. Excellentia (vivo
lume de la virtute ; sola beltà de l' unica bellezza ;
verità aperta del vero ; equale bilancia de la iustitia ;
splendida grandezza de la liberalitade ; ferma
columna de la clementia ; stabile fortezza del casto
pensiero ; lucida gemma in oro nitido e pretioso ;
amenissimo fonte in florido giardino ; micante luce
nelle tenebre ; guida, governo, albergo e habitaculo
de le nove muse) l' ho dedicato ; havendo forsi
habiuto mancho rispetto a la grossezza del mio
ingiegno e la ineptie de la lingua, che a la altezza
sua." The French translator, René Berthault de la
Grise, does not borrow or imitate this enthusiasm.
His style admits some of the vocabulary of Panta-
gruel's Limousin ; no more than the Italian's is it to
be called properly Euphuistic, though it is sometimes
under the influence of the balanced phrase :—" Et
voyant que d'assez belles matieres traictoit mesmes
pour ieunes dames l'entreprins mettre et translater
dudit ytalien en nostre vernacule et familiere langue
francoise." . . . "Et ie prie pour le surplus le plas-
mateur de la cause premiere longuement te conserver
heureuse et prospere." The Spanish sentence is
marked at once as something of a different school.

It is very doubtful how far Lord Berners went himself in approval of the antithetic pattern. His dedication of the *Castell of Love*, which is mainly from the French, is more Euphuistic than the French, chiefly through the omission of a long sentence, where the French translator having facts to state broke down into mere ordinary hazardous grammar : —" Ce petit livret iadis converty de langue castillanne et espaignolle en tusquan florentin par ung Ferraroys mon bon et singulier amy, des mains duquel en ce premier voyage que le treschrestien roy François premier de ce nom mon souverain seigneur a fait en Lombardie pour la conqueste de son estat ultramontain ay recouvert." But it remains uncertain whether or not Lord Berners ever thought much about this grammatical business : at any rate he is utterly destitute of the literary character belonging properly to Euphuists, as he never thinks it worth while to utter anything of his own, and does not ask for admiration.

There can be no question of the influence of the *Golden Boke* and the *Castell of Love* as examples of English prose. "The fysher goth not to take dyvers fyshes of the river with one baite, nor the mariner with one nette entreth into the see. I promise you the depenesse of good wylles ought to be wonne with the depenesse of the harte, some with gyftes, some with wordes, some with promises, and

some with favours." So Lord Berners translates
Guevara, and so the tune was given out for a large
company of authors who were more anxious to
profit by it than ever Lord Berners himself had
been. The *Carcel de Amor*, with its different story,
gave the same example of style :—" Dexar el camino
que llevava parecia me desvario ; no fazer el ruego
de aquel que alli padescia figurava se me inhumani-
dad ; en seguille havia peligro, y en dexalle
flaqueza," etc.

But that is not really the taste of Lord Berners.
He thinks, indeed, that prefaces and dedications
should be ornamental ; but even here, as the dedications of *Froissart* and the romance of *Arthur* prove,
when he was outside the danger of the *Castell of
Love* he chose a different kind of language. In
these prologues he makes experiments in decoration,
but they are not Euphuistic in the strict sense of the
term : that is, they do not consist in the antithetic
arrangement of phrases as that was practised by San
Pedro and Guevara. The device that falls in most
completely with his taste is that of amplification :
especially in the Prologue to *Froissart*, where his use
of triple synonyms has often been remarked—
" eschewe, avoyde, and utterly flye " ; " trouble,
sorowe, and great adversyte " ; " right profitable,
necessarie, and behovefull for the humayne lyfe."
The usage was nothing new, and it is not to be put

down to the influence of the revival of learning : it
was a piece of rhetoric common in the Middle Ages.
The Anglo-Saxon translation of Bede puts regularly
two synonyms for one word of the original,[1] and
in the course of his *Froissart* Lord Berners might
have come upon instances of triplets, as in some of
the documents quoted by Froissart :—" the sayde
thynges to holde and kepe and accomplysshe," " his
subjectes, alies, and adherentes," " our officers, ser-
geauntes, or publike persones," in " the fourme and
tenor of the letter on the peas made before Charters
bitwene the kynges of Englande and Fraunce."
Froissart himself writes :—" Comment il peuissent
prendre, eskieller, et embler villes, chastiaus, et
fortereces."

In the Prologue to *Arthur of Little Britain* the
synonyms are not scattered so freely ; and as there
is less appearance of a mechanical repetition, the
style of this piece of Lord Berners' writing has
some advantage over the others. That he should
speak of " fresshe ornate polysshed Englysshe," and
confess his failure in " the facondyous arte of
rethoryke," shows that he knew of the more
ambitious methods of composition, and that there is
something of literary criticism in his choice of
language, though he makes no great parade of it.

---

[1] J. M. Hart, *Rhetoric in the Translation of Bede*, in *An English Mis-
cellany*. Oxford, 1901.

It is evident that he does not greatly care for such
discourses as the praise of History with which he
begins his *Froissart*. He might have written more,
he says, but he was afraid that he might "too sore
torment" the reader ; wherefore he will "briefly
come to a point." His real business is with the
translation, which may stand on its own merits ; and
it is in the translation of history that Lord Berners
has done great things, in comparison to which his
small original prefaces and his divagations into the
Spanish rhetoric are unimportant.

As a translator he has many faults. Want of
scholarship is shown in all his books : he is easily
taken in by the first impression of a sentence, and
does not wait to see that it is grammar, and not
always if it make sense. For instance, in the *Golden
Boke* he is thrown out by a simple inversion, and
confounds subject and object in this way :—"I have
redde in bokes and have proved it by myselfe, that
the love of subjectes, the suretie of the prince, the
dignitie of the empire, and the honour of the
Senate, do conserve the prince, not with rigour but
with gentyll conversation" ; where the French has
"les conservent les princes" — princes keep the
love of their subjects, and so forth, not by
rigour but by affability. Some of his mistakes,
it is true, are not of his own making. The
French translator of Guevara (1531) had apparently

before Lord Berners turned *pretor en los exercitos*, "praetor in the armies," into *preteur es exercices*, which becomes in English *pretour in exercises*. The *Castell of Love*, in spite of its title-page, was evidently taken from the French version ; and if Lord Berners and his printer between them place the opening scene "in a shadowed darke valey in the mountayne called Serva de Marenus in the countrey of Masedonia," it is because the French author before him had turned the Sierra Morena into "Sierre de Moriene." Lord Berners had some knowledge of what the French books might do in disfiguring proper names, and in the Prologue to *Froissart* gives up the attempt to rectify them. He is not to be blamed indiscriminately for the cruel travesties of names in *Froissart*, though he might have done more to find out what the wonderful misspellings of the French printers really meant. Most of the names in Pynson's text are the result of an elaborate process of disfigurement. Froissart probably took some care, but he had no talent for spelling : he was content to write *l'amoureus Tubulus*, meaning Tibullus, and *Oleus* for Aeolus, and *Supernascus* for Parnassus; hence it is no wonder that English names were altered in his writing of them. Then came the copying scribes and the French printers, whose work Lord Berners had before him. *Souegne* and *Melbegue*, for Sweden and Norway, in Berners, chapter lxxiv.,

are derived from the French text, and may stand as
an example of the difficulties which the translator
found too many for him. They were increased by
the English printers, whose work was left uncorrected
by Lord Berners, and who made additional nonsense
of their own.

But apart from his neglect of the proper names,
this translator shows a want of conscience in his
attention to the meaning. Such mistakes as have
been quoted from his *Golden Boke* are found in his
Froissart also. " Thus Jaques Dartvell endedde his
dayes who had ben a great maister in Flanders ·
poore man first mounteth up, and unhappy man
sleeth them at the ende " (chapter cxv.) : this
stands for " povres gens l'amontèrent premièrement
et meschans gens le tuèrent en le par fin " ; that is,
" poor men uplifted him at the first, and wicked men
slew him in the end." " Par eschielles de cordes et
gravés d'acier " — " rope-ladders and steel - grap-
plings "—is translated " with helpe of the archers."
Achier, the spelling in the text which he was using,
was enough to set him on this bold but unnecessary
and misleading version, which rather confuses a
spirited account of an escalade, though it is picked
up and well continued after this :—" And first there
entred, raumpynge uppe lyke a catte, Bernard de la
Salle, who in his tyme hadde scaled dyvers forter-
esses," and so on.

IV

It is difficult to exaggerate the merits of Froissart as a narrator, taking a reasonable view of his circumstances and intentions. But it is possible to praise him wrongly. It is well understood now that much of the fame of the *Chronicles* is due to Jean le Bel, the real author of the greater part of the First Book ; and apart from those large debts that can be verified by a comparison of Froissart with the recovered history of Jean le Bel, there is much in the common estimate of Froissart that is really due to the Middle Ages in general, and the traditional spirit of story-telling of which Froissart had his share. His forms of composition are inherited, and other writers have described before him all the pageant of which he is the accomplished master : the movements of armies, the shock of battle, the valour of this knight and that knight, and how they severally bore themselves in the press, and so forth. So far from being singular in his command of stories, Froissart appears as one of a numberless multitude of historians, who have all of them Froissart's interest in events, and in various degrees the power of setting them out in a narrative. Instead of admiring Froissart, one is often inclined to wonder at the commonness of this gift of story-telling ; and when Froissart is praised for his sieges, adventures, ambushes, and all the rest of it, there crowd into the court where he is getting his reward, who shall say how many captains, voyagers, chaplains, and common soldiers with journals and memoirs that might stand along with Froissart's Cressy, if spirited actions, described as they took place, be what is wanted in a chronicler? Of all the things in literature for which grace is to be said, there is none that is at once so plentiful in quantity and so inexhaustible in attraction as this kind of writing. It flourishes in any season and any climate. The Epic may wither and the Tragedy fail, but there is seldom want of the good bread of Chronicles, Journals, Memoirs, Narratives, whatever they may be called, and there is as little weariness in them as in any things composed by men. The shortness of life may perhaps have its advantages, as various philosophers have explained ; but it leaves a regret that there is hardly time in any ordinary life for all the memoirs of France. And there are other languages, even the despised medieval Latin, as Carlyle discovered in his Jocelyn of Brakelonde. The writing in Jocelyn's *Chronicle* is not so good as Froissart's ; but if mere lively sketching of an incident be what is wanted, why should not Jocelyn claim his own ? Those who wish to see past things as they were, will think as fondly of the streets of St. Edmund's Bury, and the old wives protesting against taxes with their distaffs, as of the

Court of Gaston de Foix in Froissart's *Chronicles*.
At least they will not care to stop and choose between
one and the other. Jocelyn of Brakelonde lets them
have a picture of something happening, and again,
as Carlyle has sufficiently brought out, he can give
the impression of a person's character and how it
strikes a contemporary ; and what can Froissart or
Horace Walpole give more? Many things, no
doubt ; but not things of the same essential, satisfy-
ing flavour as the picture of events, in which the
monk of St. Edmunds, and many a ship-captain in
Hakluyt, might compete with Froissart ! The gift
of narrative, like the gift of courage, is always and
everywhere something near a miracle ; but these
miraculous qualities are pretty widely distributed
among the human race. Perhaps the tendencies of
education and culture have been rather to conceal
the merits of the chroniclers by directing attention
to moralists and philosophers instead ; also the beaten
ground of Livy, and the school historians writing
mechanical sentences with the ablative absolute, are
known to have produced an unfortunate aversion
from history which has probably checked explorers.
Dr. Johnson, who was sick of the Second Punic
War, would surely have found the medieval
chroniclers as well worth reading as the romances
in Dr. Percy's library. He was not a friend of
Gray, or he might have been guided differently ;

but, as it was, Gray had few companions in his taste
for the historians of chivalry. The love or the
respect for great authors has naturally left out of
notice the simple authors who make a record of
events in any grammar that comes handy. The
absorption of the schools in science, and abstract
philosophy, and the pretensions of the moral essayists
(with half a dozen historical examples in their stock
to enliven their account of human nature), prevented a right appreciation of old chronicles.
Hence, the brilliancy of Froissart, who happens to
be generally known or at any rate famous, has
perhaps been too emphatically acknowledged, with
too much isolation of Froissart from the other
French historians, and also with not enough recogni-
tion of the common and widespread faculty of good
story-telling. Froissart has been praised for what
belongs to Villehardouin, and for qualities that he
shares with any one who has been in lively places and
can give an account of them, or who can repeat with
spirit the stories of adventure, or even of mere commonplace occurrences, that he has heard from others.
It would be easy to find in any age of literature any
number of brilliant passages of narrative and description in writers who have no pretence to fame as historians. Perhaps one must except the great classical
ages of Greece and Rome ; for the ancients, or the
Fates on their behalf, seem to have cleared away the

less successful writers to let Homer and Herodotus live at ease in their room. But the Gothic Ages have been less thorough in their pruning ; and from the days of St. Jerome to the last soldier's letter about this year's war there is an endless supply of the kind of history that stirs the reader of Froissart. It is very commonly disregarded by most of the human race, and perhaps most of all by the best educated, but it has its reward. When a chronicler of this kind is read for the first time, he has the same effect as Baruch had on La Fontaine. The discoverer goes about asking his friends : " Have you read Jocelyn of Brakelonde ? " Because Jocelyn has worked a miracle for him, in showing him visions of the past and things as they actually happened ! The praise of Froissart, the stock comparison to Herodotus, might have provoked opposition before this from the friends of the less famous writers. Have you read Giraldus Cambrensis ? or Galfridus Malaterra ? or Dino Compagni ? Have you read Pitscottie ? Do you know the real character of King Stephen, as shown when he sat playing at " chevaliers " with the boy William, that was afterwards Marshal and Earl of Pembroke ? Do you know the youth of Mark Alexander Boyd, " playing the loon on the Sabbath Day," and waiting at night in the Glasgow street to have the life of the Professor whose discipline was not agreeable ? The Professor, Mr. James Melville,

has given his account of this part of the Renaissance
in his *Diary*, and of other things as lively. Is
his impression of what happened, and his record of
it, less vivid than Froissart's ?   Has Froissart anything truer, anything more courteous, more absolutely
sufficient in every way, than Melville's interview
with Don Juan Gomez ?   Froissart in such things is
equalled by his two chief predecessors in French
history, to name no more. He does not come
nearer to the very truth of the thing than Villehardouin. The approach to Constantinople and the
thrill of apprehension and resolution mingling at
the sight of the place they had come to take, the
chief city of the world, the solemnity of this, the
sudden revelation of the place, and the immediate
shock of surprise, all the difference between what
you have thought about and what you see before
you, Villehardouin has put into one magnificent
sentence :—

Quant il virent ces haus murs et ces riches tours dont
ele estoit close et ces riches palais et ces hautes yglises dont
il avoit tant que nus nel péust croire s'il ne le véist propre-
ment à l'ueil, et il virent le lonc et le lé de la vile qui
de toutes autres estoit souveraine, sachiés qu'il n'i ot si
hardi à qui le char ne fremesist : et ce ne fu mie merveille
s'il s'en esmaierent, quar onques si grans afaires ne fu
empris de nulle gent puis que li mons fu estorés.

And as much in his own different way has been done
by Joinville.   Among the shadows and the bodiless

voices of the House of Fame, the knights of Mansourah, as Joinville saw and remembered them, are still possessed of their human life and their own proper character. There is Count Peter of Brittany, hustled from the field by his men, and showing how little he thought of them as he spat the blood from his mouth and cursed them; holding on to the saddle-bow to keep the rout from unseating him :— "Bien sembloit que il les prisast pou." And among all the many good things that have been said on the battle-field, from the days of Sarpedon downward, we may doubt whether anything is better than the speech of the good Count of Soissons :—"Li bons cuens de Soissons, en ce point là où nous estiens, se moquoit à moy et me disoit : Seneschaus, laissons huer ceste chiennaille ; que par la Quoife Dieu ! (ainsi comme il juroit) encore en parlerons nous entre vous et moi de ceste journée ès chambres de dames."

Froissart has also gained credit for a simplicity and directness of style which is really common to his age, to all the Middle Ages, more or less. This is very pleasantly brought out by one of his French editors, who chanced to be drawn to Froissart not in the ordinary way. M. Buchon did not take up Froissart at first because of Froissart's reputation as a medieval historian : he had read other historians first, in Portuguese ; it was from admiration of

Fernan Lopes, he says, that he turned to look for something corresponding in his own language, and so came upon Froissart. But with most readers the case is different. They have not read Fernan Lopes, perhaps no medieval prose at all, and they are apt to take as the peculiar beauty of Froissart that charm of simple phrases which belongs even to the weakest medieval writings in the vulgar tongue, to the *Petit Artus*, to the *Reali di Francia*, and not exclusively to the great books like the *Quest of the Holy Grail*.

There is as wide an interval between the masters and the botchers in the thirteenth or the fourteenth century as at any other time, and Froissart is as far removed from the incompetent medieval proser as Gibbon is from Russell's *Modern Europe*. But there is this difference : that, while the useless prose of later times is neither fit for the land nor yet for the dunghill, there is generally something even in the feeblest of medieval writings which has not wholly lost its savour,—something that attracts even a man of the eighteenth century, as Dr. Johnson was taken captive by *Palmerin of England*. It does not belong to the great books only, to Froissart or Malory ; but even the commonest hackwork of chivalry has a power of attraction in some of its phrases. All the weariness, all the respectability of well-educated books are unavailing with a certain class of readers if they only hear such opening words as " Or dist li contes," and "Now torne we fro this mater and speke we of Sir Tristrem." Phrases like these kill the phrasing of modern historians—*e.g.* "the arts as well as arms of his subtle enemy," or "foiled in his design, the weak but unscrupulous monarch," etc. If you test this sort of good grammar along with common phrases such as may be found easily enough at any opening of the books of chivalry—"Now shewethe the story that anone, after that Huon was enteryd into the chapell"—it is certain that some readers will consider this last the more admirable. What is beyond question is, that the dulness of the Middle Ages is redeemed by that grace of simplicity, and by the command of phrases that even in the poorest context yet bear witness to their gentle ancestry. Medieval prose calls up the thought, at any rate, of something different from the grammar-school ; and the grammar-school, with Holofernes for its teacher, is what is suggested by most of the polite literature that has been composed since the Renaissance, once its day is over.

Of all the languages French had gone furthest in tuning the common medieval prose to effects of pathos, making the most of the contrast between deep meaning and innocent-looking words. No language written by grown men ever comes near the old French in giving a tone to narrative like the awe-stricken voice of a child. The old French

writers must appeal to you for pity and wonder,
must call out "how great the loss," and add in the
next breath, "but there was no help for it, so they
had to let it be" ("mais amender ne le porent").
In old French literature the individual strength or
levity of a writer's character seldom does much to
modify this hereditary trait of style; the most
worldly and the strongest minded talk in this way;
there is little irony known, and tears come quickly
to the eyes over the common fortunes of the race.
Jean le Bel and Froissart are gentle-hearted men,
in different degrees, and both of them were poets
and lovers of romance. They use this sort of
language, and they use the formulas of romance
to bring a thing vividly before the mind :—"He
that had seen this, had been filled with wonder."
"Qui donc veist hommes, les femmes et enfans de
chiaus plorer et tordre leurs mains et criier à
haulte vois très amèrement, il n'est si durs coers ou
monde qui n'en euist pité" ; — "There was nat so
hard a hert if they had sene them but that wolde
have had great pytie of them" :—so the sorrow of
Calais is represented by Lord Berners, cap. cxlvi.,
but he does not convey the full association of the
original phrase with the formulas of the heroic poetry.
"Là véisiés fier estor esbaudir" ;—"there might
you see fierce stour of battle raging, lances shivered,
shields broken, the coats of mail torn through and

rent." It was in such phrases of the *chansons de geste*
that the earliest French historians learned their ways
of appealing to an audience. And it is the epic
manner again that has determined the fashion of a
sentence like this in the beginning of one of the
chapters on Cressy :—"Ceste bataille, ce samedi,
entre la Broie et Creci, fu moult felenesse et très
horrible." It is used again for Najera in 1367 :—
"Che samedi au matin entre Nazres et Navaret";
and it recalls the magnificent opening of the old heroic
poem in the cycle of William of Orange :

A icel jor que la dolor fu grans
Et la bataille orible en Aliscans.

It has the epic way of making the time and the place
seem notable, as if they partook in the action. Such
is the habit of the old French writers of history.

V

The most probable date of Froissart's birth is
1338 ; his life [1] is nearly contemporary with Chaucer's.
Between the fortunes of the two writers there are
many close resemblances : Froissart appears to have
been, like Chaucer, sprung from a prosperous townsman's family, and, like Chaucer, he found it not

[1] The *Life* of Froissart, by Mme. Darmesteter, in the series of
"Great Writers of France," has made it easy to follow his career, and
not so easy to say anything fresh about it.

difficult to get access to courts and noble houses.
He had not Chaucer's imagination, nor his full sympathy with different conditions of men, but his birth
and his good temper saved him from the exclusive
preference of courtly and chivalrous affairs that
has sometimes been attributed to him. A man of
Hainault, a townsman of Valenciennes, had no right
to look down upon respectable burgesses. In the
notes on his own life in his poems he makes no
pretence of great dignity for himself : he takes
something like the humorous view of his own
modest rank that Chaucer presents in the *House of
Fame* and in the interludes before and after *Sir
Thopas*. Froissart coming back from Scotland, with
his one horse Grisel carrying him and his saddle-bag,
is a traveller of less magnificence than Jean le Bel,
and there is no affectation of courtliness in the confessions of the *Dit du florin*, how his money went in
the taverns of Lestines. There was not the sharp
division between knights and burgesses that is sometimes supposed—for example, in Claverhouse's description of him to Henry Morton. Eustache de
St. Pierre, of the town of Calais, is one of the
heroes of Jean le Bel and of Froissart, and Froissart
notes the death of a " valiant burgess of Abbeville "
in a "brunt" of battle in 1369,—"the which was
great damage,"—just as if he had been a knight.

He has given an account of his schooldays and

his early love affairs in the poem of *l'Espinette amoureuse*. This is his *Vita Nuova* ; but while Dante's story is made as solemn as the prophetic books that he quotes in it, and filled with the quintessence of the old idealist worship, Froissart's poem varies easily between the formulas of the allegorical tradition and a literal account of the way he spent his youth in Valenciennes, from the time when his amusements were like those of Gray at Eton or Cowper at Westminster to the incidents of his unsuccessful courtship. The fourteenth century was quite capable of such personal notes and such urbane confessions as are common in less " Gothic " periods. Froissart was a memoir-writer as well as an author of songs and virelays. His " mémoire ymaginative," as he calls it in the *Trésor amoureux*, was employed in his own small adventures at school, before he turned to the chronicles of the " Prowess " of Christendom.

The record of his life contains little besides his travels and his literary works, the travels being generally for the sake of his history. He went to England in 1361 to present a book of his to Queen Philippa, and spent about five years at the English Court. In 1365 the Queen sent him with good credentials to Scotland. He stayed fifteen days at Dalkeith, in the house of the Earl Douglas, and saw there his son, the Douglas who fell at Otter-

bourne : "a fair young child, and a sister of his called
the lady Blanche." In his account of Otterbourne,
Froissart mentions that in his youth he had ridden
"nigh over all the realme of Scotland"; King David
took him with him on a progress through the
country, and he "searched all the realm to the
wild Scots." In his travels he noted not only such
things as were told him about Robert the Bruce
and about the manners of the Scots (to verify Jean
le Bel's descriptions), but also, more fancifully, the
names that he used in composing the scenery of his
tale of *Meliador*, such as Snowdon, which is the name
of Stirling in romance. On his return, which is the
subject of one of the pleasantest of his shorter poems,
he seems to have spent some time with the young
Lord Despencer, whose father-in-law, Bartholomew
Burghersh, comes often into his story. Passages of
conversation with Despencer are among the additions
made by Froissart to his last redaction of the First
Book. They have not the same extent as his report
of the talk on the way to Bearn in 1388, but they
are significant : Despencer pointing out the towns
that his family had lost through "the ill queen."
Froissart was at Berkeley Castle along with him in
1366, and heard the story of it from an old squire :
he asked questions, he says, to "justify" his history.
Then he went to Brussels, where he was befriended
by Wenceslas of Brabant for the sake of Queen

Philippa, and then to the Black Prince at Bordeaux. He was at Bordeaux on Twelfth Night, 1367, when Richard, son of the Black Prince was born ; and, being known as a chronicler, was bidden to write down the fact for his book. After a short visit to England again, he went out along with Despencer to accompany Lionel of Clarence to his wedding at Milan. The journey had a bad ending in the death of the bridegroom not long after the marriage. Froissart went on to Rome, about which he has nothing to say. He seems to have preferred Stirling, in his "Gothic" taste. Queen Philippa died in 1369, and Froissart came back to his own country of Hainault, where he must have worked hard at his *Chronicles*, with such diversions as are indicated in the *Dit du Florin*, a poem written twenty years later. In an earlier poem, *le Joli buisson de Jonece*, which dates itself the 30th of November 1373, he gives a pleasant account of his own fortunes and of those who have befriended him : Queen Philippa, the Duchess Blanche of Lancaster, for whose early death he makes his lament, Isabel, Lady of Coucy, her father King Edward, her husband (Sir Enguerrand), and many others ; the Duke and Duchess of Brabant, the Duke Aubert, the three lords of Blois, Lewis, John, and Guy, especially Guy ; the Count Amadeus of Savoy ; last of all, his Scottish friends, whom he ought to have

mentioned before — the King, and the Earls of
Douglas, Mar, March, Sutherland, and Fife :

> Haro ! que fai ! je me bescoce
> J'ai oublié le roy d'Escoce
> Et le bon Conte de Duglas
> Avec qui j'ai mené grant glas :
> Bel me reçurent en leur marce
> Cils de Mare et cils de la Marce
> Cils de Surlant et cils de Fi.[1]

He does not here mention Robert of Namur, for
whom the First Book was composed.

Froissart set out on his adventures when he left
Hainault for England in 1361, to offer to Queen
Philippa his first essay in history :—" Howbeit I
took on me, as soon as I came from school, to *write
and recite* the said book, and bare the same compiled
into England, and presented the volume thereof to
my lady Philippa of Hainault, noble queen of
England, who right amiably received it to my great
profit and advancement." Berners does not quite
rightly give the original meaning : — " Ce non
obstant si emprins je assez hardiement, moy yssu de
l'escolle, *à dittier et à rimer* les guerres dessus dites."
The book presented to the Queen of England was
not any part of the present *Chronicle*, but a rhyming
history, such as are found in plenty, though this one
of Froissart's is lost.[2] It was doubtless in the

---

[1] *Buisson de Jonece*, l. 363 *sq.* (Scheler, *Poésies de Froissart*, t. ii.
p. 11).

[2] Something has been saved : thirty-six octosyllabic verses on the

ordinary verse of romance, such as was used in the *Life* of William the Marshal long before this, and in Chandos Herald's *Life* of the Black Prince later ; and in a book that claims remembrance in connection with Froissart and Jean le Bel, by John Barbour, the historian of the Bruce. Froissart had from the first the right historical sense that made him go about asking questions and taking notes, but he was not at first, apparently, drawn to the methods of Villehardouin and Joinville. He preferred the old mode of utterance, in rhyme : as in the days when prose was not thought fit for a gentleman to read, or rather to have read to him. Prose was enjoined upon him when he made up his mind to continue Jean le Bel, and to sacrifice his first attempt, or at any rate to disregard it. What happened to his plans is clearly enough explained in his Prologue, though it is not clearly brought out by Berners. He had, of his own motion and through his natural interest in the subject, gathered material for a history of the wars of England and France, chiefly about the battle of

events of 1357, apparently from Froissart's poem, have been found in two parchment slips used for binding, and published by M. L. Delisle in the *Bibliothèque de l'École des Chartes*, LX. pp. 611-616. M. Longnon, in calling attention to this at the end of the third volume of his *Meliador* (p. 368), observes that it is most probably this early historical poem of Froissart's which is mentioned in the library catalogue of King Charles V. :—*La guerre du roy de France et du roy d'Angleterre, et les faiz du roy de Navarre et de ceulz de Paris quant ilz furent contre le roy . . . escript en françoys de lettre formée, et rymé, a deux colombes.*

Poitiers and what followed, for the earlier history was rather too far back for his own memory to serve him well. This history he compiled into metre and presented to the queen. Then, as he went on with his researches, he found that it would not stand, and that he had not rightly made out the actors in the story and their proper exploits. He had the motive of heroic literature strongly at work in his mind— namely, the desire to honour the great deeds of champions in war ; and he found that somehow or other his rhyming chronicle had gone wrong or come short in its attribution of glory to the different knights. So he fell back on the *Chronicles* of Jean le Bel of Liége, made these the foundation and the first part of his work, and continued them, starting in his new undertaking from about the time when he may have begun to suspect and criticise the book presented to the queen, which was about the time when Jean le Bel comes to an end :—" Therefore to acquit me in that behalf and in following the truth as near as I can, I, John Froissart, have enterprised this history on the foresaid ordinance and true foundation, at the instance and request of a dear lord of mine, Robert of Namur, knight, lord of Beaufort, to whom entirely I owe love and obeisance, and God grant me to do that thing that may be to his pleasure."

The life of Froissart is determined by the favour

of his patrons, and so are his opinions. This has
been shown most clearly by M. Siméon Luce in his
investigation of Froissart's ways of working and the
processes by which the different redactions of his
First Book were brought about. The English sympathies of the First Version (which is the most
popular in manuscripts, and which was taken as
material for the early printed copies, and therefore
was translated by Lord Berners),—the English
accounts of Cressy and Poitiers,—are due to Froissart's attachment to the English party in his early
life, to the favour of Queen Philippa, and the pro-
tection of Robert of Namur. Robert of Namur
came back from journeys like those of Chaucer's
Knight in Pruce and the Holy Land, and offered
his services to King Edward at Calais in 1346 ;
although he was not constant altogether in his
support of the English, he was more for that side
than for the French. Froissart dedicates to him the
First Book of the *Chronicles*, written from the
English point of view. But before 1373, when he
became curate of Lestines, under the patronage of
Gui de Blois, Froissart's opinions began to change.
Queen Philippa had died in 1369 ; he had come to
be more and more closely drawn to the court of
Brabant, where Wenceslas of Bohemia, husband of
the duchess, gave his countenance to Froissart, and
made him the confidential friend to whom he gave

his poems. Wenceslas, son of King John of Bohemia who fell at Cressy, naturally had other sympathies in connection with the war than those which Froissart had represented ; while Gui de Châtillon, Count of Blois, was nephew of that saintly Charles of Blois who had died at Auray (cap. ccxxvi.), maintaining his right in Brittany against the English supporters of the rival claim, and his father too had died at Cressy on the French side. For Gui de Blois the Second Redaction appears to have been made between 1376 and 1383 : it is found in two manuscripts, the chief of which, at Amiens, is thought by M. Luce to have been copied from Froissart's own writing, and from writing done in haste and not very easy to read. Gui de Blois, a good knight, who was hostage in England when King John was set free from his captivity, who like Robert of Namur had made journeys in "Pruce," who fought against the English in Guienne, and commanded the French rearguard at Roosebecke in 1382, was the chief patron of Froissart in the rest of his life : the Third Book was written about 1390 for his good master and lord, Gui, Count of Blois, and in the Prologue of the Fourth Book Froissart describes himself as "chaplain to his dear lord above named," as well as treasurer and Canon of Chimay and of Lille in Flanders. Gui de Blois died in 1397, before the *Chronicles* came

to an end, and before the last redaction of the
First Book.

Froissart probably drew away from Robert of
Namur owing to a coolness between Robert of
Namur and Wenceslas in 1371 ; down to the death
of Wenceslas in 1383 Froissart was his friend and
associate in poetical studies. His romance of
Meliador, long lost but now recovered, and lately
published, was written to introduce in it the lyrics
of Wenceslas—poems for which Mr. R. L. Steven-
son's review of Charles of Orleans has said by
implication everything most to the purpose. Their
music is the thinnest that human senses can appre-
hend, yet they are true and graceful in their own
way, though there is no substance in them. Their
author was gently born, and the piety of Froissart was
well bestowed in honouring and preserving his poems.

The First Book was finished about the time when
Froissart went to Lestines, about 1373 ; it was
revised for Gui de Blois (the Second Redaction)
between 1376 and 1383, and in these years and
later Froissart was occupied with his Second Book,
great part of which is the chronicle of Flanders.
After 1381, when Gui succeeded his brother John as
Count of Blois, Froissart was made his chaplain and
became Canon of Chimay. Between Blois and the
Low Countries he saw some more of the world, and
towards the end of 1388, in order to get fresh

material, he made the journey to Bearn that rightly takes up so much room in his memoirs and in every account of his life and character.

Froissart's Third Book begins[1] with the matters, from 1382 onward, that he learned at Orthez in 1388, concerning " the business of the realms of Castile, Portugal, Navarre, and Aragon, yea, and of the realm of England and country of Bourbonnois and Gascoyne." In telling about these things he gives not only the substance but the way in which the stories came to him in his journey southward, and also the conversations at the house of " the high and mighty prince Gaston, Earl of Foix and Bearn." He brought with him his romance of *Meliador*, containing the poems of Wenceslas of Brabant,—" the songs, ballads, rondels, and virelays which the gentle duke had made in his time,"—and read the book aloud for the night's entertainment. Apart from historical criticism, no comment on this part of Froissart's life can do much more than repeat his own story, and that is unnecessary : his story may be read in its proper place, as he wrote, or as Lord Berners has translated it. There is no need for any chorus to the tragedy of the house of Gaston Phœbus —" the piteous death of Gaston, the earl's son,"— and as little for the less solemn passages, where Froissart told the story of Acteon, as possibly help-

---

[1] At the xxi. chapter of Berners' Second Volume (1525).

ing to explain the strange disease of Sir Peter of
Bearn, or where he listened to the squire's tale " how
a spirit called Horton served the lord of Corasse a
long time, and brought him ever tidings from all
parts of the world." From this date his manner
of writing history changes : there is more of his
personal memoirs, a greater freedom of discourse
and of digression. It was not that he acquired new
powers, or that he learned the art of making his
journal interesting ; for his poems, it will be found,
show much the same faculty of dealing with personal
matters as the conversations of Orthez, and Froissart
had of course from the first been a writer of
reminiscences. But he certainly increased his
freedom ; and, when he went back in his old age
to revise his First Book, he added many circumstances " beneath the dignity of history," and gave,
for example, not only the results of his early inquiries in England, but in some cases the way in
which his researches were carried out : for instance,
in the talk with Despencer already quoted. And
his later visit to England is recorded, not in the
style of the First Book, but like the visit to
Orthez : the conversations are fully reported, and
the circumstances noted. Besides the information
given by Sir Richard Stury at Eltham, it is told, in
one of the memorable expressions of Froissart's
quick sense for what was about him, that he and Sir

Richard were walking up and down in the shade of
a vine-trellis, while his old acquaintance of four-and-
twenty years back explained to him the condition
of England. Unfortunately this sentence did not
come into Lord Berners' *Froissart* :—" Et toutes les
parties qui sont icy dessus contenues, celluy vaillant
chevallier anchien messire Richard Stury les me dict
et racompta mot à mot en gambiant les galleries
de l'ostel à Eltem où il faisoit moult bel et moult
plaisant et umbru, car icelles galleries pour lors
estoient toutes couvertes de vignes."

Froissart throve at Orthez : the generous life
there and the favour shown to him and to his book,
" the *Meliador*," gave him an exhilaration that does
not seem to have passed away. He left Orthez in
March 1389 in the train of the young Duchess of
Berry. At Avignon (where he lost his purse) he
wrote the *Dit du florin*, a poem about himself and
his own fortunes, in which he shows the same kind
of spirit as in his prose memoirs of the same date.
On his way back to Hainault he met his old friend
and patron, " mon tres chier et grant seigneur," he
calls him, " monseigneur Enguerran Seigneur de
Coucy," whose life and fate (after Nicopolis) were so
well in harmony with the legendary sorrows and the
chivalrous reputation of the name he bore. From
Enguerrand de Coucy he got news of English affairs.
After a visit to Valenciennes and to Gui, " the Earl

of Blois," he returned to Paris in time to see the entry of Queen Isabel on Sunday the 20th of June 1389 ; he gives a very full account of all the shows, pageants, and devices made in her honour. Later, at Bruges, he collected Portuguese intelligence from Don John Pacheco, and finished his Third Book, the whole of which must have been written at high pressure and with great zest and spirit. In 1390 the Fourth Book was begun, and dedicated, like the others, to Gui de Blois. But Gui de Blois was not quite able to keep all Froissart's old devotion. He died in 1397, ruined by extravagance and " accidie," having had to sell his estate of Blois ; and the latter part of the *Chronicles* is somewhat overcast by the shadow of his decline. He is not mentioned among the patrons whom Froissart consulted before his visit to England in 1394. Froissart applied for aid and countenance to Albert of Bavaria, Count of Hainault, Holland, and Zealand, and Lord of Friesland, to his son William of Ostrevant, to the Duchess of Brabant, and to the Lords of Coucy and of Gommegines. Gui de Blois is remembered at his death as an honourable lord who had been liberal in his help to Froissart and in his encouragement of the *Chronicles*, but before his death his wealth had shrunk, and the historian had to turn elsewhere for a patron. There was nothing exactly disloyal in this, and Albert of Bavaria was no new friend to Froissart ; but all the

same there is something rather sad in the passing of
Gui de Châtillon and in Froissart's acceptance of the
new conditions. Albert of Bavaria and his son
were Knights of the Garter, and attached to England
in their sympathies, and Froissart had begun to
think again of a still older debt than that which he
owed to Châtillon—his obligation to Queen Philippa
and her children. He returned to England in July
1394.

Naturally in this visit there was the common
disappointment; the old nests had other birds in
them. At Canterbury Froissart stood by the tomb
of the Prince of Wales; he had not seen Richard,
King of England, since the day when the child was
held at the font in the church of Bordeaux. His
old acquaintances were mostly dead. But he found
Sir Richard Stury, whom he had seen last in 1370 at
the court of Wenceslas at Brussels, and he was well
received by the king, who accepted graciously his
richly bound and jewelled volume of poems,—"in
a fair book, well enlumined, all the matters of
amours and moralities that in four and twenty years
before I had made and compiled." There is no
attempt in these chapters of Froissart to keep
merely to public history. It is in this part of his
memoirs that the passages occur to which Gray calls
attention in his letter to Wharton (January 23,
1760) :—" Pray, are you come to the four Irish

Kings, that went to school to K. Richard the 2d.'s Master of the Ceremonies; and the man who informed Froissard of all he had seen in S. Patrick's Purgatory?" Froissart in England in these latter days heard the grumbling of the nation, from Thomas, Duke of Gloucester, down to the populace of London, against the misgovernment of the king; and he takes notice in his own way of the same things as were expressed in a different manner by his contemporary, the alliterative poet, in his complaint and admonition to Richard the Redeless. He left England late in 1395. Not much is known of the rest of his life. He appears to have lived mostly in his own country of Hainault, working at his books. His history ends tragically, with the ruinous defeat at Nicopolis, and with the death of King Richard. But this was not the last of his memoirs. After 1400, though he did not continue his history beyond the accession of Henry of Lancaster, he went back again to the First Book, and began re-writing it in an original way, making his own that part of his *Chronicles* which had mainly been due to Jean le Bel. This revision— the Third Redaction, extant in the one manuscript of Rome—goes down to 1350, and is very different in style from both the other versions. The tone, which in many places had been flattened a little through the transference of Jean le Bel's original narrative to the copy of his work in Froissart, is now freshened again by means of digressions, remarks, and reminiscences of Froissart's own. The earlier history comes out in this last version more impressively through Froissart's indignation and distress at the fall of King Richard ; the character of the English nation as he describes it in the manuscript of Rome is determined by what he had himself observed, not in 1365, but thirty years later. Nothing definite is known of Froissart after this, and the year of his death is uncertain.

VI

The French poets of the fourteenth century, the masters and the contemporaries of Chaucer, have not received the same attention from literary historians that has been given to the earlier medieval schools. No one has set himself to explain and characterise them as M. Gaston Paris and his pupils have described the triumphs of the thirteenth and the fourteenth centuries, the Arthurian Romances, *Reynard*, the *Fabliaux*, the early lyrical poetry of France, the *Romaunt of the Rose*. And they are still too medieval — Guillaume de Machaut, Eustache Deschamps, and Froissart — for the professors of modern literature, who regard the Middle Ages as merely a preserve for philologists and antiquarians, and who find that one *chanson de geste* is the same as another, and none of them really worth much notice from an educated taste or a serious historian. Fortunately the texts of these poets have not been neglected, though their value has not been fully estimated for the history of literature. One can form one's own opinion, with the scholarly editions of the poetry of Froissart and of Eustache Deschamps, easily accessible as they are, and with Chaucer's earlier poetry to help one to an understanding of their motives. Nor should the essay of M. Sandras be omitted,[1] in which he tries to reduce Chaucer to the rank of a mere dependant on his French instructors, and does no harm to Chaucer thereby, while he illustrates Machaut and Deschamps, and gives a clue to some of the mazes of that Garden of the Rose in which the French poets were fond of walking.

All the poets of that school were servants of the Rose, believers in the *Romaunt of the Rose*, and their office might be regarded as a kind of lyrical variation or descant on the themes given out in the authoritative text of Guillaume de Lorris, from which, as from a perennial fountain, their jets of ballades and virelays are refreshed and supplied :

> The God of Love, a ! *benedicite*,
> How mighty and how great a lord is he !

---

[1] *Étude sur G. Chaucer, considéré comme imitateur des trouvères.* Paris, 1859.

These poets, with Chaucer in his youth, are of the household of that lord, and find their way to his Garden in the dream of a May morning ; and their poems have the dreamy charm of the place, so indescribable, yet so distinct even from the things that are most like it, such as the Provençal poems, or those of Petrarch, which are akin to the Rose indeed, but not in the same close degree as the makings of Machaut, Froissart, and Chaucer. This common bond of loyalty, however, does not explain everything in that fellowship of poets, and Froissart, like Chaucer, has more than one way. It has perhaps been too often and too hastily taken for granted that in the French school of the fourteenth century there was nothing more than the lyrical repetition of the old conventional amatory motives in the form of ballades, rondels, and *chansons royales*, having great beauty of poetical form, in narrow limits, but without variety or novelty apart from the systems of the rhythms and the rhymes. If there had been nothing more, there would still have been Chaucer's *Complaint to Pity* and " Hyd Absolon thy giltë tresses clere " ; and also that most exquisite deliverance of Chaucer's finest poetical sense, the lament of Anelida. But there would not have been the dialogue in the *Parliament of Birds* ; and even the *Book of the Duchess*, closely as it conforms in most respects to the tradition of the Rose, is not altogether a dream.   It is not strange that Chaucer should very early have found the ways of the French tradition too strait for him.   But the French authors also, though they had not the same poetical career before them, are free to go beyond the limits of the Rose ; the poetry of Froissart and Deschamps, if there be nothing in it like the Canterbury Pilgrims, is at least as free as the *Parliament of Birds* or the *House of Fame* ; and besides the beauty of their ballades and rondels (which any churlish classical person may disparage if he choose) there is an amount of humorous and satirical poetry that is hardly recognised by those who think the Middle Ages wanting in the modern qualities of wit and worldly elegance.   The passages where Froissart tells things about his own life are as sound, as clear, as free from "Gothic" encumbrance as even Swift's autobiographical verses.   What is most of all to our purpose, they illustrate the *Chronicles*.   The motive of Froissart in the *Chronicles* is not altogether purely the love of exploits and prowess or the desire to praise famous men.   Happily, in many parts of his work, especially in the latter part of the *Chronicles*, as has been seen, the memoir-writer gets the better of politics and the art of war, and reveals the true extent of this theme, which is nothing less than human experience as understood and remembered by himself.   Froissart declares himself at last in the

chapters on his visit to Bearn, so very different from
the history of the wars. In the first part of his
work he does not talk about himself, and report
conversations with the same fulness. He does not,
unluckily, report the talk by the way during his
visit to Scotland as he does the conversations with
Sir Espaing de Lyon on their journey to Orthez.
The earlier notes are given without their setting.
Stirling and Dalkeith and the evening's entertainment
there are not described in the same manner as the
nights at Orthez in the house of the Count of Foix.
The new method that he adopts for 1388, and had
not used for 1365, is not to be ascribed merely to
"the tattling quality of age," nor yet altogether to
a maturing of his style, an enlargement of his scope,
a growing freedom from the dignity of history.
No doubt there was a development of this sort
going on : he felt that there might be enough of
battles, sieges, and ambuscades ; why should he not
indulge his genius ? But his genius had found its
way before this in the memoir notes that he put into
various poems, and his poems show him as he really
is more intimately than the more important historical
pieces of his *Chronicles*,—a man pleased with the
recollection of anything that has happened to him,
an average good-humoured Epicurean temperament
quickened into something finer by his sense of a
continuous excitement in the mere process of living,

and with a gift of expression in which his memoirs shape themselves for narrative. The short poem on his horse Grisel and his greyhound coming back from Scotland is a specimen of Froissart's mind. It is like a poem for a child, telling how the horse and the dog exchanged remarks on life and on their master. "See what hard work I have," says the horse, "with so much to carry, while you run free!" "But consider," says the greyhound, "how well our master cares for you, how he goes to see that you are fed, how you are given a comfortable lodging and a bed of straw or fern, while I am tied up at the door or anywhere to keep watch"; and so on. In all which, besides the fluent verse, there is nothing remarkable, except that Froissart on his travels should have amused himself by thinking into rhyme the common trials of his companions — he was fond of animals — and the common charities of the road. There is no heightening nor idealising nor ornamentation of the subject; nothing much more than a pleasant appreciation of what is happening about him in an ordinary day's journey; without any epithet or any poetical diction he draws toward his inn. Froissart has set down in verse, using his horse and dog to speak for him, his record of the fact that his heart leaps up when he beholds the church spire at the end of the day's stage, and knows that it means an inn not very far off. This is outside the allegorical garden, and it reveals the same good-tempered and frank enjoyment of life that carried Froissart through so much. Life is generally so interesting to him that he has no time to be wearied. Though the mass of his writing is large, it never looks like task-work. *Tristitia* was one of the Seven Sins for which he had no inclination. Hence his writings move most easily ; he is never preoccupied, and has always time to spare. The romance of *Meliador*—which, to be sure, is not a very substantial work, for all its length—would seem to have been turned out as a sort of amusement, a relaxation from the claims of history. In the same way that other good-natured man, Froissart's contemporary, Boccaccio—" John of the Tranquillities "—might lapse into Tuscan verse or prose as a relief from his serious labour at the Genealogy of the Gods or the history of the Falls of Princes. Chaucer was less mercurial than his French and Italian compeers, and shows more sign of study in his writings, and less levity. But Froissart, Chaucer, and Boccaccio deserve to be remembered together in honour of the century in which they lived as the three great writers who have least of the writer's melancholy.

At the first glance there is a temptation to think of Froissart's poetry and his *Chronicles* as roughly corresponding to the difference between Chaucer's earlier and later poems : as though the *Chronicles* and all Froissart's historical researches implied the same kind of turning towards real life, the same kind of discontent with the shadows of the Rose, as may be found in Chaucer's literary progress—in the difference between the *Complaint to Pity* (for example) and the Canterbury *Prologue*. Froissart, we might imagine, like Chaucer, grew weary of the allegorical landscape and the visionary actors, of Beau-Semblant, Bel-Accueil, and Franc-Vouloir, even of the heroes and heroines, Paris and Helen, Tristram and Iseult, "Polixena et Dame Equo," and the other gentle ghosts of the *Lovers' Paradise*. But this anticipation is hardly borne out by the facts of Froissart's nature or the succession of his works. It is not exactly true of Chaucer that he ever gave up anything : the pageant of the *Legend of Good Women* is later than the strong life of his *Troilus and Criseyde*. Of Froissart it is even less to be affirmed that he intentionally withdrew from the artifice of the fashionable poetry because he was tired of it and wanted something more real to break his mind upon. His occupation (or his diversion) with the romance of *Meliador* shows that he kept up both interests at once. But besides this it has to be remembered that the courtly school itself allowed its poets to deal pretty freely with real life. The rules of their Paradise were not so strict as in the time of

Tannhäuser : they could go in and out much as
they chose. It is easy to distinguish the poems or
the parts of their poems in which they keep to the
full ritual of the old observance of the Rose, and
again the poems where cheerfulness is seen breaking
in, where the light is daylight, where the tone is
that of urbane conversation, or at least as near it
as was possible for a fourteenth century author of
moral essays in verse. In the scope of his poetry
Froissart is not very different from Clément Marot.
The wit and good humour of poems like the *Dit du
florin* are the proper things for what was originally
called Satire by its Roman inventors, and the old
Horatian tag upon Lucilius, the Boswellian motto, is
not out of place in connection with the poetry of
Froissart ; for though much of it belongs to the
schools of the medieval amorists, its character as
a whole is rather that of confessions, impressions,
notes, and criticisms of life :

> Quo fit ut omnis
> Votiva pateat veluti descripta tabella
> Vita senis.

His poems got some share of his confidences, his
prose memoirs had the rest, and the life of " Sir John
Froissart of the country of Hainault " is shown in
them like a picture.

VII

The original author of most of Froissart's First Book is Jean le Bel, canon of St. Lambert of Liége, who, according to the chronicler Jean d'Outremeuse of the same city and of the canon's household, " placed great care and all good diligence in this matter, and continued it all his life as justly as he could, and much it cost him to collect and gain it." Jean le Bel died about 1370, over eighty years old. Along with his brother Henry he took part in the expedition of Jean de Beaumont in 1327, which brought him to York, Northumberland, and Scotland, along with the army of King Edward. He appears in Berners (cap. xv.) as "syr John de Libeaux," among the Hesbegnons of Hesbaye.

Jean de Hemricourt, in the *Miroir des nobles de Hesbaye*, gives an account of Jean le Bel and his way of life that shows him to have possessed the virtue of magnificence, besides his faculty of writing sound history. He was one of the most splendid persons of his time, " of frank and noble conditions, and richly dressed," " grand et hauz et personables de riches habits et stoffes," with ermine, sendal, and precious stones ; " the fashion of his house was this, and he had in this way instructed his squires of honour, that without consulting their master, if they saw any gentle stranger, whether prelate or knight or

squire, they invited him forthwith to dinner or
supper, and any prince who visited Liége was brought
to dine with Jean le Bel. When he went to church
on holidays there was as large a following as for the
Bishop of Liége, forty or fifty in his train, who all
came to dinner with him afterwards ; he was looked
up to as their head by his kinsfolk and friends,
and took care of their advancement. He had good
natural sense and good demeanour more than most
men ; he was blithe and gay and glad, and could
make songs and virelays, and followed mirth and
pastime ; and in this course of life he obtained both
heritages and pensions. By the grace of God he
lived all his days in prosperity and good health, and
was more than eighty years old when he died, and
according to his rank were his obsequies reverently
and costly carried out. He left great possessions to
two sons—twins—named John and Giles, who were
born to him when he was old of a damsel of good
family belonging to the house of Des Prez." The
description of Jean le Bel's magnificence might make
one a little anxious about his talent for literature—
it is consistent with florid tastes ; but of these there
is no sign in his *Chronicles*, and his narrative has less
affinity with the ermine and sendal and the rich display of his household than with the habits of warfare
which he learned in following his lord Jean de Beaumont. His client, Jean de Hemricourt, has said not

a word too much in praising the liberal mind of his master : Jean le Bel had a clear head and a frank bearing, and his *Chronicles* are not affected by any touch of vainglory. He had imagination, among other things, and was a lover of heroic poetry ; though it is not so pronounced as in some of the earlier French historical prose, there is in Jean le Bel the tone of the epic language, the phrasing of the *chansons de geste* ; it has been noted also in Froissart. In Jean le Bel's expedition in England with John of Hainault the places that belonged to King Arthur gain his attention, and he is pleased when he writes the name of " Carduel in Wales which was in the days of Arthur," or " a white abbey which in the days of King Arthur was called the *Blanche Lande*," and again, " the castle of Windsor that King Arthur built, and where the Table Round was first established." He remembers the famous sieges made by Charlemagne, Alexander, and Godfrey, and compares the valour shown at Neville's Cross to that of Roland and Oliver. He has the same motive as Froissart in bringing out the prowess of good knights and in recording the *grans apertises d'armes*. At the same time his judgment is unclouded by any of the magic mists of romance ; the vigour of his story is not sophisticated, and indeed his story was begun in a sort of protest against the marvellous exaggerations of common minstrels, the "jongliours et en-

chantours en place," as Froissart calls them in his
reference to Jean le Bel's antipathy for their fables.
He writes for "persons of reason and understanding," *gens de raison et d'entendement*, in order to
displace the *bourdes controuvées*, "the multitude of
words invented and repeated to embellish the rhyme,
and the crowd of wonderful achievements told of
certain knights and other persons," all out of measure,
and more likely to discredit the subjects of them by
their impossibility than in any way to do them
honour. This pursuit of a true method is justified
by the talents of Jean le Bel ; his praise of "sooth-
fastness" is by no means a conventional opening or a
hackneyed depreciation of rival authors. Nor does
it mean anything prosaic or dull : such things are
far removed from the generous heart whose ways
were described by Jean de Hemricourt. He is the
author of some of the best known and most highly
honoured things in Froissart : the chapters on the
surrender of Calais and the devotion of Eustache de
St. Pierre, and on the death of the Bruce. He
wrote the often-quoted account of the Scots and
their warfare, from his own observation ; and
Froissart, though he studied the same subject on the
same ground, did not cancel the report of Jean le
Bel in favour of any newer notes of his own. One
chapter he struck out, because he would not believe
it true ; but true or not, it remains as one of the

P

finest things in old French prose—the tragic story
of the Countess of Salisbury, the dishonour of King
Edward, and the sentence spoken on him by the
wronged earl, more lofty, more magnanimous, and
more impressive in its power of condemnation than
the revenge taken upon Tarquin.   Jean le Bel, who
can use with good effect the ordinary easy con-
versational language of medieval French chroniclers,
can also rise to the height of a tragic argument in
phrases of as much severity and dignity as any
Roman author would have found appropriate for
such a theme.

Froissart has left out other things also which are
worth reading in the original Chronicle.   Jean le Bel
has a character of his own ; and though Froissart's
editing is most judicious for his own purposes, it is
not quite the same thing as Jean le Bel speaking in
his own person.   Jean le Bel was at York in 1327
and Froissart was not ; so naturally there is a
difference in the two versions.   Froissart keeps
everything that he can, but he cannot keep the
directness and immediate force of the older historian's
remarks on what he actually saw :—" Incontinent
after dinner there began a great fray between
some of the grooms and pages of the strangers
and the archers of England who were lodged
among them in the said suburbs."   Froissart gives
all this, but he cannot speak of it as Jean le Bel

goes on to do :—" And I myself, who was there present, could not enter my lodging to arm me, myself and my companions, so many English did I find about our doors in a mind to wreck and plunder at large ; and we saw the arrows flying so thick upon us that it behoved us to withdraw to another place and wait the event along with the others." And "we fell into the hatred of all the country except the great lords ; the people hated us worse than the Scots who were burning their country." The narrator who can say "we" has an advantage over one who says "they" ; and Jean le Bel, who saw the smoke of the Scottish fires with his own eyes, is worth listening to apart from Froissart. The smoke of an invading enemy seems to have dwelt in his imagination, for he brings it in vividly in his account of 1346, and Froissart here has not kept the touch that emphasises the weakness of the French king :— " How was it that King Philip who was at Paris a bare seven leagues away, with all his power of lords and men at arms that he had summoned for defence of the country,—how was it that he did not fall upon those enemies who were making their smoke and flames fly over his head in Paris, or why did he not at least defend the passage of the river ? "

Jean le Bel's criticism of the two kings is also left out by Froissart, but it is a fine piece of historical censure. Room may be found for it here, not simply

as an historical note on the matters contained in the
First Book of Froissart, but rather to show the
independent value of Jean le Bel's historical judgment and his gift of plain speaking :—

Some who shall hear this history read will wonder why I
call the King of England "the noble King Edward," but
the other simply "King Philip of France"; so they might
think and imagine that I maintained a side and a party.
With due respect, I do not write thus out of party leanings,
but I do it to honour him who in this history bears himself
most nobly : that is the noble King Edward, for whom no
honour is too great ; for in all his needs he has always taken
good counsel, and listened to his people, knights, and squires,
and honoured each in his degree, and well defended his
realm against his enemies, and made large conquests upon
them, and ventured his own body at home and forth of his
realm along with his men unwavering, and has well paid his
soldiers and allies, and freely given of his own : therefore he
ought to be willingly served by all and everywhere have the
name of noble king. Not thus has the King of France
acted, but has let his land in many marches be exiled and
wasted, and has in all places kept himself so as to ease his
person and keep from danger ; and has always trusted poor
counsel of clerks and prelates, and even of those who said to
him, "Sir, be not dismayed and run no risk of your life, for
hardly will you guard against treason ; who can tell that
any man is loyal ? But let this young King of England
waste his time in folly and spend his substance ; his smoke
will not take the kingdom from you, and when he has spent
all he must go back ; he has not yet conquered Boulogne,
Amiens, or Saint Omer ; when he is gone you may easily
make good your losses." Such counsellors King Philip
followed, not the lords and barons of his country ; but some
he put to shameful death, and their heirs disherited. The

less should be his praise and honour among all men. Withal, he sore oppressed his country under taxes, and the churches with tithes, and forged bad money in different places, and again called it in and uttered better, and again debased it, so that in trade there was no certainty. And the soldiers were never well paid, but often had to spend of their own, in fault of payment, and also had often to sell their horse and armour before they found the paymasters. A prince who thus behaves himself ought to have the less love from his men ; and it is great pity and loss when by ill counsel the realm of France that had surmounted all the world in honour, wit, learning, chivalry, merchandise, and all good things is thus tormented and to this mischief brought by its enemies and itself, that he who ought to be lord of it is captive, and nearly all the lords and knights of the land are dead or in prison. Verily I believe it is by miracle that God suffers it so to be. And now I will leave off, I can say no more than this, and will return to our matter to speak of the noble King Edward, whom all should love, praise, and honour, for well he has deserved it ; God be praised. (Chap. LXX.)

The recovery and publication of Jean le Bel's authentic work[1] is a gain not so much of new material for French history as of an author with a mind and style of his own, who now has his proper place among the masters of the French tongue. He has not the variety nor the wide range of Froissart. But he writes like a man of honour and a man of good sense, acquainted with great affairs and able to find the right words for them.

[1] *Les Vrayes chroniques de Messire Jehan le Bel.* Edited in two volumes by M. L. Polain : Brussels, 1863.

Incidentally, and apart from the matter of his book, Jean le Bel will always be interesting through the contrast between the quiet tone of his narrative and the apparent pomp and glory of his manner of living. It must perplex a moralist to find this very unaffected story coming from a man of such splendid ways as those described by the clerk of Hesbaye ; while it might also puzzle an economist to explain how the revenue of Jean le Bel was increased under those conditions, which look so much like mere ostentation and prodigality. Such resolution and independence are not easily found in so rich a house. The contrast is like that in the case of Chaucer's Monk, from whom, as he is described in the *Prologue*, one would not expect the " Tragedies " that he afterwards recites, nor the gravity of his mood and disposition.

VIII

Froissart's *Chronicles* have been found wanting in many respects, and their credit has been damaged in several places by exact historical criticism ; but these blemishes, even from the scientific point of view, are small in comparison to his merits and the great amount of news of all sorts that he has collected and exhibited. Was it possible for him to have done more than he did by way of "justifying" his history ? The wonder is that he could have done so much, when we consider what a great mass of writing is published as his work, in prose and verse. And not all of his work is extant. There was hardly time for him to do more. Between his researches, his taking of notes, his composition of new chapters for his *Chronicles*, and his revision of old work, besides his songs and virelays, his moral poems, and the leisurely romance of *Meliador*, he can seldom have been idle. He was not negligent, though he may have made mistakes ; and it is hard to see how he could have spent his time better than he did, if he was to accomplish the enormous labour he had set himself to get through.

Was he the historian of a declining age, of false chivalry ? He has been so represented, but it is not easy to accept this opinion about him. He is spoken of sometimes as if his *Chronicles* were a romance of chivalry, without substance or gravity, as if all the life in it were a pageant or a tournament. But is this really so ?

Froissart has the French character of the fourteenth century. He notes, by the way, that the English think every one French who uses the Gallic tongue ; but although he would not call himself French, there is no injustice in giving him the common qualities of the French courtly authors in the time in which he lived. French literature in the fourteenth century had undoubtedly not a little vanity in it. The court poetry of Froissart and his contemporaries, including Chaucer, was living on ideas and imaginations that had begun to lose their youth and freshness even before the days of Guillaume de Lorris, a hundred years and more before Froissart was born. The motives of the old French heroic romances were exhausted, and *Meliador* is the dream of a shadow ; the old lyric motives of Provence and of the Provençal schools in other languages had been repeated for generations before the poets of ballades and rondels adopted new metrical forms without changing the spirit or the common ideas of the old tradition. *Meliador*, both in Froissart's narrative couplets and in the rondels and virelays of Duke Wenceslas, is all reminiscence and repetition of conventional common forms, and *Meliador* is a representative book : if one wishes to know what chivalrous poetry had come to in 1380, it is to be found there. It has graces indeed, but there is no strength in it. The strength of poetry is elsewhere at that time,—in the Italian study of classical literature and in Chaucer's following of the Italians.

But this does not dispose of Froissart's *Chronicles*, and even Froissart's poetry, it has been seen, is not all convention and repetition. It is true that in many respects his age was one of literary exhaustion, and it is true also that Froissart remained all his life insensible to the chief new sources of literary strength

that were accessible in his time : he had no interest
in what was being done in Italy, and in spirit he came
no nearer to his contemporary Petrarch than if they
had been living in separate worlds or with a thousand
years between them.   Italy made no impression on
him when he travelled there, and is incomparably less
valuable to him than Spain, which he had never seen.
He notes the fortunes of Sir John Hawkwood and
his companies in Italy, and some of the business of
the Papacy, and with some detail and in his best
manner the rise of the Visconti at Milan ; but he
did not know nor care what Petrarch and Boccaccio
were about, and he brought back from his Italian
travels nothing in the smallest degree resembling the
acquisitions of Chaucer.   He was made for the world
he lived in ; and the meteors that were flickering
here and there as intimations of a change that was
drawing on, the restlessness, the misgivings by which
the spirit of Petrarch was disquieted, had no effect
on Froissart, and lay beyond his consciousness.
Froissart's soul was at ease :

> Coer qui reçoit en bon gré
> Ce que le temps li envoie
> En bien, en plaisance, en joie,
> Son eage use en santé,
> Partout dire l'oseroie.[1]

These moral sentiments of Froissart express his own

---

[1] *L'Espinette*, l. 1021 ; *virelay*.

mind thoroughly : he took in good part whatever
Time sent him, and spent his life happily—quite at
home in the world where he found himself.   No one
would go to him for anything like those intimations
of vast unachieved discoveries in literature such as
perplex and disturb the life of Petrarch, "dreaming
on things to come," and make him what he is for
every one who has been drawn under his influence.
If Froissart had known the letters of Petrarch he
would not have liked nor understood them ; he
would have dismissed them with another of his
moral verses, in which the old proverbial judgment
is reiterated against those who look for better bread
than is made of wheat :

> C'est grant folie de querir
> Meilleur pain que de bon froment.[1]

But if Froissart, compared to Petrarch, be wanting
in depth and originality, wanting in perception for
anything beyond the ordinary ranges of life, it is not
just to put him down as limited or partial in his treatment of his own proper ground.   If his work be
superficial,—and this is what is alleged against
him, — at any rate there is a good extent of
surface, and many things come into the picture
besides the vainglory of the age of chivalry.   To
judge from some accounts of him, one might imagine

[1] *Trésor amoureux : Poésies,* Ed. Scheler, iii. p. 161.

that there was a tournament on every second page, and that the matter of the *Chronicles* was the same as that of *Meliador*, where indeed the vanities have their own way, and ample room to display themselves. The knight-errant, it is true, is there, as he is in Chaucer's *Prologue*, come back from Pruce or Gernade. But Robert of Namur or Guy of Châtillon is no more fantastic than Chaucer's Knight; and as for tournaments, if they are a sign of decay, then the age of chivalry was already far gone long before this, for tournaments are made more of in the sober biography of William the Marshall than in Froissart's *Chronicles*. When it is said that Froissart writes as if the whole of life were one long holiday for lords and knights, is there not some confusion between the temper of the historian and the things he writes about? Undoubtedly Froissart takes the whole of life with enjoyment, and his *Chronicles*, in spite of the falls of princes, are not depressing to read. Nor is the *Decline and Fall of the Roman Empire* : it was written by an historian with the same invincibly happy temperament as Froissart. But the contented minds of Froissart and Gibbon do not misrepresent the facts by leaving out afflictions and distresses. Though Froissart may be kept alive for his fifty years of chronicle-writing by an equanimity of nature that protects him from the strain of tragic emotions and from melancholy, and though his demeanour, like Gibbon's, may be too placid for readers with a taste for gloom and fire in historical pictures, he does not cover up the miseries of life or cry peace when there is no peace. It is not a theatrical or unreal life in his pages : it is not the less real because it is showy in some of its aspects ; and most of the fighting in it is not showy, but grim enough. Froissart is no more ostentatious with his banners and pennons waving in the wind than the Books of Moses are, when they go into details about knops and bowls and lavers, and ram-skins dyed red. And much of the warfare in Froissart, as in Jean le Bel, is chivalrous just in the sense that any war may be chivalrous where there is courage and heroism. It would not be grossly misleading to say of Froissart that life as he represents it is all ambuscades and surprises, hungry and heavy marching in pursuit of invisible enemies, all weariness, wounds, death, and captivity of good knights. The end of Chandos was rather wretched : " he slode and fell down at the joining with his enemies," and a squire gave him his death-wound with a stroke coming on his blind side, for he had only one eye. The Captal died in prison, and Sir Enguerrand of Coucy broken-hearted in captivity among the Turks, after he had seen the butchery at Nicopolis, the most pitiful and shameful ruin of the best knighthood of Christendom.

It would be easier to prove Froissart a writer of sad stories than a chronicler of the false splendours of chivalry, if one were set down with his book before one to find illustrative passages by turning over his pages. William Morris in his poems from Froissart (in the *Defence of Guinevere* volume) has discovered more of the spirit of his history than the professed historians who complain of his levity and cheerfulness. Froissart, it is true, does not dwell too long on themes like those of *Sir Peter Harpdon's End* or *Concerning Geoffrey Teste Noire;* but he knows the cruelty of war, and if he had wanted knowledge of such griefs, and of the way human beings are wrung by them, he might have learned from Jean le Bel's heroic work what such things are. But he did not need this instruction.

Froissart's wars are no doubt influenced by the chivalrous ideal, which counted for something in the life of the fourteenth century. Don Quixote, if he had lived in the time of Chaucer's Knight, would have been considered sound in his principles and not remarkably extravagant in his manner of expressing himself. He might have justified himself by the example of the English knights-bachelors in 1337, who went to win their ladies' grace in the fields of France, each with a patch over one eye. He might have quoted the companion of Ywain of Wales, on the French side in 1369, who was commonly called the Pursuivant of Love. King John of France founded the Company of the Star, which was to be like the Round Table of King Arthur ; and Chandos and a French lord disputed before Poitiers because "each of them bare one manner of device, a blue lady embroidered in a sunbeam above on their apparel." But if this be vanity, it is not all that Froissart has to tell : the battle of Poitiers was a real battle, and not a mere thing in a story-book. Froissart understands the gentlemen who went into war "their bodies to advance," to win honour ; but it is no design of his to turn them into absolute romantic knights. Froissart, who could write verse about a small boy making dams in running water at Valenciennes, was not offended by real things, and never tried to alter the reports he got (from James Audley and others) in order to make his *Chronicles* look more like the adventures of *Meliador*. He shows no preference for the kind of fighting which is most like tournaments. Joinville praises a battle in which there is nothing but clean strokes in the mellay, no interference of bolts or arrows ; but Froissart knows many different kinds of fighting, and does not disparage any of them for the sake of that which was of course the noblest. His great captains and his other valiant men are not reduced to the abstract type of chivalry. Bertrand du Guesclin is perhaps not treated with full

justice by Froissart, but at any rate he is one of the
"prowest," and he is very different from the conventional romantic hero. Froissart understands the
practical hard-working military man, from Edward
the Black Prince, Sir Walter Manny, Sir John
Chandos, Bertrand du Guesclin, Oliver Clisson, to
the less eminent ranks of Sir Robert Knolles and Sir
John Hawkwood, and lower than these the chiefs of
brigands, Bacon, Crokart, Geoffrey Teste Noire, and
Aymerigot Marcel. The adventures are varied, the
men engaged in them are not all alike.

Froissart's story resembles Barbour's in many
places—not only where they are telling of the same
matter in the same order, as in the scene of the
death of the Bruce, but where the same kind of
incident is found in different places. The "sleights"
of Barbour are like the "subtilties" of Froissart,
especially where there are fortresses to be taken.
Any one who has been told that Froissart is all
tournaments and vanity should read the story of
the ingenious person who won the city and castle
of Evreux, "the which as than was French," in
Berners, cap. clxxvi. : how he talked pleasantly to
the captain and got into the castle, with authentic
news that the kings of Denmark and Ireland had
made an alliance and were going to destroy all
England. It might have had a place among the
"interludes and jeopardies" of the Bruce, along

with the story of William Bunnock at Linlithgow
or the " trains " made by Sir James Douglas.

Some of the liveliest of Froissart's episodes did
not find their way into the vulgate text, and so did
not reach Lord Berners.   One of these is the game
of chess between King Edward and the Countess of
Salisbury ; another is the story of Oliver de Mauny
at the siege of Rennes.   They are worth considerably
more than most commentaries and criticisms, and
the readers of Froissart may be left to form their
own judgment upon them, as upon the rest of the
book to which these omitted chapters belong.   This
is the story of the king's game of chess.   In
Berners, cap. lxxvii., it reads, " All that day the
kyng taryed ther," and so forth, with nothing about
the game.   From that point the fuller version goes
on as follows, unhappily not in the English of Lord
Berners :—

After dinner the tables were removed.   Then the king
sent lord Reynold Cobham and lord Richard Stamford to the
host and the companions who were lodged under the castle
to know how they did, and that they should make ready,
for he wished to ride on and follow the Scots, and that they
should send on all the carriages and the munitions, and by
the evening he would be with them.   And he ordered the
Earl of Pembroke to make the rear-guard with five hundred
lances, and that they should wait for him on the field till
he should come, and all the rest should ride forward.   The
two barons did all as he commanded.

And he remained still in the castle with the lady, and

hoped that before his departure he would have response more agreeable than he had had as yet. So he called for chess, and the lady had it brought in. Then the king asked the lady to play with him, and she consented gladly, for she made him all the good cheer that she might. And well was she bound thereto, for the king had done her a fair service in raising the siege of the Scots before the castle, and again she was obliged because the king was her right and natural lord in fealty and homage. At the outset of the game of chess, the king, who wished that something of his might be won by the lady, challenged her, laughing, and said, "Madam, what will your stake be at the game?" And she answered : "And yours, sir?" Then the king set down on the board a fair ring that he wore with a large ruby. Then said the countess, "Sir, sir, I have no ring so rich as yours is." "Madam," said the king, "that which you have, set it down, and consider not so narrowly."

Then the countess to please the king drew from her finger a light ring of gold of no great worth. And they played at chess together, the lady with all the wit and skill she could, that the king might not hold her for too simple and ignorant ; and the king played false, and would not play as well as he knew. And there was scarce pausing between the moves but the king looked so hard on the lady that she was all put out of countenance, and made mistakes in her play. And when the king saw that she had lost a rook or a knight or what not, he would lose also to restore the lady's game.

They played on till at last the king lost, and was check-mate with a bishop. Then the lady rose and called for the wine and comfits, for the king, as it seemed, was about to depart. And she took her ring and put it on her finger, and she would fain have had the king take back his own again, and presented it to him and said : "Sir, it is not meet that in my house I should take anything of yours, but

Q

rather you should take of mine." "Nay, madam," said
the king, "but the game has made it so, and if I had won
be assured that I should have carried yours away." The
countess would not press the king further, but went to one
of her damsels, and gave her the ring, and said : "When
you shall see that the king has gone out, and taken leave of
me, and is about to mount his horse, do you go forward and
render him his ring again, courteously, and say that in no
wise will I retain it, for it is not mine." And the damsel
answered that so she would readily do.

At this the wine and the comfits came in. And the
king would not take of them before the lady, nor the lady
before him, and there was there a great debate all in mirth
between them. Finally it was agreed, to make it short,
that it should be together, as soon the one as the other.
After this, and when the king's knights had all drunk, the
king took leave of the lady, and said to her aloud, so that
no one should comment upon it : "Madam, you abide in
your house, and I will go to follow my enemies." The
lady at these words courtesied low before the king. And
the king freely took her by the hand and pressed it a little,
to his contentment, in sign of love. And the king watched
until knights and damsels were busy taking leave of one
another ; then he came forward again to say two words
alone : "My dear lady, to God I commend you till I
return again, praying you to advise you otherwise than
you have said to me." "My dear lord," answered the
lady, " God the Father glorious be your conduct, and put
you out of all base and dishonourable thoughts, for I am
and ever shall be ready to serve you to your honour and
mine."

Then the king went out of the room, and the countess
also, who conveyed him to the hall where his palfrey was.
Then the king said that he would not mount while the lady
was there, so to make it short the countess took her full and

final leave of the king and his knights and returned to her bower with her maidens. When the king was about to mount, the damsel whom the countess had instructed came to the king and knelt; and when the king saw her he raised her up very speedily, and thought that she would have spoken of another matter than she did. Then she said: "My lord, here is the ring which my lady returns to you, and prays you not to hold it as discourtesy, for she wishes not to have it remaining with her. You have done so much for her in other manners that she is bound, she says, to be your servant always." The king, when he heard the damsel and saw his ring that she had, and was told of the wish and the excuse of the countess, was all amazed. Nevertheless he made up his mind quickly according to his own will; and in order that the ring might remain in that house as he had intended, he answered briefly, for long speech was needless, and said: "Mistress, since your lady likes not the little gain that she won of me, let it stay in your keeping." Then he mounted quickly and rode out of the castle to the lawn where his knights were, and found the Earl of Pembroke waiting him with five hundred lances and more. Then they set out all together and followed the host. And the damsel returned and told the king's answer, and gave back the ring that the king had lost at chess. But the countess would not have it and claimed no right to it: the king had given it to the damsel, let her take it and welcome. So the king's ring was left with the damsel.

The story of Oliver de Mauny at the siege of Rennes, and of John Bolton and the partridges, belongs to 1357, and would have appeared in Berners, cap. clxxv., where he gives the coming of the young bachelor "Bertrande of Glesquyne," but not of his cousin :—

And there were newly come to the siege two young bachelors, cousins german, who were afterwards much renowned in the realm of France and the realm of Spain, as you will hear further on in this history. These two cousins were named Bertrand du Guesclin and Oliver de Mauny. And the said Bertrand during the siege fought in single combat with an English knight, likewise renowned, called Sir Thomas Dagworth; and the combat was appointed for three courses with a lance, three strokes of an axe, and three strokes of a dagger. And these two champions acquitted themselves valiantly to their great honour; howbeit the said Bertrand gave such a stroke of his axe to the said Englishman that he smote him to the ground with violence. And there it ended. And they were eagerly watched by those within and also by those without: then they left the field without great hurt to either. So the Duke Henry of Lancaster kept his siege before Rennes a long time, and made many assaults, but nothing gained there.

Now it happened one day during the siege that an English knight, Sir John Bolton, a man of valour in war, had been for sport to the fields with his sparrowhawk, and had taken six partridges. He mounted his horse, armed at all points, with his partridges in his hand, and came before the barriers of the city and began calling to the townsmen that he wished to speak with Sir Bertrand du Guesclin. Now it chanced that Oliver de Mauny was standing above the gate to watch the condition of the English host; and he perceived and was aware of the Englishman with his partridges, and asked him what he wanted and whether he would sell or give his partridges to the ladies who were in the place besieged. "By my faith," answered the English knight to Oliver, "if you dare bring your bargain nearer and come and fight with me, you have found your chapman." "In God's name," said Oliver, "yea, wait for me and I will pay you on the nail." Then he came down from the walls to the ditches, which were all full of water, and plunged in and swam, and crossed them, armed at all points save the harness of the legs and his gauntlets, and came to his chapman who was waiting for him. Then they fought, valiantly and long, and quite near to the host of the Duke of Lancaster, who looked on well pleased, and forbade any one going forth to them. And also those of the town and the ladies who were there took great delight in watching them. The two valiant men fought on, and the end of it was that Sir Oliver de Mauny overcame his chapman, Sir John Bolton, with his partridges, and carried him off without his leave and sore wounded across the ditches and into the town, and presented him to the ladies with the said partridges, and they received him gladly and did him great honour.

It was not long afterwards that Oliver felt his wounds paining him sore, and could not get the herbs that he knew would cure him. So he called upon his prisoner courteously and said: "Sir John, I am hard wounded; and I know some herbs out there which with the help of God would cure and restore me. Now, I will tell what you shall do: you shall go out from here and go to the Duke of Lancaster your lord, and bring me a safe-conduct for myself and three men for a month till I am healed; and if you can obtain it for me I will let you go free, and if not, then you will return here to be my prisoner as before." At this news Sir John Bolton was well pleased, and went away to the English court, where he was gladly welcomed by all, and by the Duke of Lancaster no less, who rallied him well about the partridges. And then he made his request and the Duke granted it, and gave him the safe-conduct written and sealed. Sir John returned at once with the safe-conduct, and gave it to his captor, Sir Oliver de Mauny, who said that he had done admirably, and forthwith freed him from his captivity. And they set out together from the good city of Rennes

and came to the host of the Duke of Lancaster, who was
glad to see them, and received them heartily and showed
great kindness to Oliver. And the Duke said that he had
a noble heart, and proved that he would yet be a valiant
man and of great prowess, "when to get my safe-conduct
and a few simples he had released a prisoner who might well
have paid him ten thousand florins of gold." After this the
Duke appointed a room to lodge Oliver de Mauny, and
ordered it to be richly hung and furnished, and every one to
give and afford him all that he might require. There was
Oliver housed in the camp of the Duke, and the surgeons
and physicians of the Duke attended him and visited him
every day; and also the Duke came often to see him and
cheer him. And he stayed there and was healed of his
wounds; then he took his leave of the Duke of Lancaster,
and thanked him much for the great honour he had done
him; and also he took leave of the other gentlemen and of
Sir John Bolton, his prisoner that had been. But at his
going the Duke of Lancaster gave him some fine plate in
a present and said to him: "Mauny, I pray you commend
me to the ladies, and tell them that we have often wished
for partridges for them." With this Sir Oliver departed
and came to the city of Rennes, where he was joyfully
received by every one great and small, and by the ladies, for
whom he had plenty of news; and more especially to his
cousin Bertrand de Guesclin he told the whole of his
adventure, and they had much mirth of it between them,
for they loved one another well, and afterwards till their
death, as you shall hear recounted later in this story.

Chaucer was harder than he need have been to
the two cousins in his Monk's *Tragedy of Peter of
Spain* : whatever "cursedness" they may have brewed
later for the ally of the Black Prince, this episode

would make one think well of Mauny, "wicked nest"
though Chaucer calls him.   Another passage of
Chaucer comes to mind in another way to illustrate
the history of Froissart : the battle of Actium in the
Legend of Cleopatra, saint and martyr, has its companion, if not its original, in Froissart's sea battle at
La Rochelle on St. John's Eve, 1372 (Berners, cap.
ccxcvii.-ccxcix.), when the Earl of Pembroke was
taken.   The Spaniards are not said to have thrown
pease on the hatches to make them "slidder," as was
done at Actium ; but the nature of the business is
the same in both, and no more and no less chivalrous
in either than the affair of the *Shannon* and the
Chesapeake.

Description with Froissart is seldom employed for
the mere sake of ornament.   He has not in his
prose, and not very noticeably in his poetry, the
common taste of the Middle Ages for elaborate catalogues of furniture and minute descriptions of works
of art, such as the sculptures at the beginning of the
Romaunt of the Rose, or the pictures of the *Æneid* in
Chaucer's temple of Venus in the first book of the
House of Fame.   When he takes up this kind of
work, as in the pageants for the queen's entry into
Paris in 1389, he does it with a will, but he does not
introduce such things irrelevantly.   Generally it will
be found that where he is most brilliant with his
scenery and properties he is also most dramatic :

they accompany the action, and do not impede one's view of it. He is very particular about the way things appeared on the blazing day when King Charles VI. fell into his frenzy (Berners, II. clxxxvii.) :—

The French King rode upon a fair plain in the heat of the sun, which was as then of a marvellous height, and the King had on a jack of black velvet, which sore chafed him, and on his head a single bonnet of scarlet, and a chaplet of great pearls which the Queen had given him at his departure, and he had a page that rode behind him bearing on his head a chapeau of Montauban bright and clear shining against the sun, and behind that page rode another bearing the King's spear painted red and fringed with silk, with a sharp head of steel ; the Lord de la River had brought a dozen of them with him from Toulouse, and that was one of them ; he had given the whole dozen to the King, and the King had given three of them to his brother the Duke of Orleans and three to the Duke of Bourbon.   And as they rode thus forth the page that bare the spear, whether it were by negligence or that he fell asleep, he let the spear fall on the other page's head that rode before him, and the head of the spear made a great clash on the bright chapeau of steel.   The King, who rode but afore them, with the noise suddenly started, and his heart trembled, and into his imagination ran the impression of the words of the man that stopped his horse in the forest of Mans, and it ran into his thought that his enemies ran after him to slay and destroy him, and with that abusion he fell out of his wit by feebleness of his head, and dashed his spurs to his horse and drew out the sword and turned to his pages, having no knowledge of any man, weening himself to be in a battle enclosed with his enemies, and lift up his sword to strike, he cared not where, and cried and said : " On, on upon these traitors ! "

Here no doubt an educated taste would blame the excessive notice of particulars, as Dante was criticised by Warton for relating things " circumstantially and without rejection." But Froissart does not always write so vividly, and here the circumstances are given " without rejection," because he is leading up to the event that gives them all their right proportion ; his mind is not like that of the conventional poets who were accustomed to put in a description of a king's pavilion or of pictures in a hall when they could not think of anything better to fill out their story. Froissart's descriptive passages are not the lazy intervals in his history, like the pauses for orna- mental catalogues of precious things in the old French romances, not to speak of other and more classical kinds of poem. Froissart's mode of descrip- tion varies with the dramatic interest of the scene— taking " dramatic " to mean generally whatever belongs to the action. He is never still for a moment. He does not put down blocks of inani- mate detail between his passages of adventure. His writing is made what it is principally through his sense of time—that is, his sense of the way things change their appearance as the plot develops itself. There is another chapter which shows this plainly enough : the description of Edward III., as admiral,

waiting for the Spanish fleet in 1350—an addition of
Froissart's own to the matter he borrowed from Jean
le Bel, and an example of the strength of his early
work even before he had come to rely entirely on his
own materials.　Unfortunately this did not come
into Lord Berners' copy, the early French editions
having a bad text about that part, confused, abridged,
and padded with extracts from other chronicles:—

The King of England, who was at sea with his fleet,
had given order fully for all that was to be done and for the
manner of engaging the enemy, and had made my Lord
Robert of Namur captain of a ship, which was called
La Sale du Roy, where all his household was.　And the
King sat on the quarter-deck of his ship, wearing a jack of
black velvet, and on his head a black beaver hat that became
him well.　And as I was told by those who were with him
that day, he was as merry as he had ever been in his life, and
made his minstrels play before him a dance of Almayne
that Sir John Chandos, who was with him, had newly
brought over.　And further for his pastime he made the
said knight sing to the minstrels' music, and took great
delight in it.　And ever he looked aloft, for he had set a
watch in the topcastle of his ship to give warning when the
Spaniards came on.

Now when the King was taking his pleasure thus, and
all the knights very glad to see him of such good cheer,
the watch that saw the Spaniards heave in sight said:—
"Ho! I see a ship, and it looks like a ship of Spain."
Then the minstrels ceased; and he was asked if he saw
more.　Not long after he answered and said, "Yes, I see
two—and three—and four."　And then when he saw the
main fleet:—"I see so many, God help me, that I cannot

tell them all." Then the King and his people knew that it was the Spaniards. Then he bade sound his trumpets, and all their ships drew in to be more in order and better for defence, for they knew that they should have battle since the Spaniards came in so large a fleet. By this time it was late, upon the hour of vespers or thereabout ; and the King called for wine and drank, as also did all his knights, and put his basnet on his head, and so did the others.

Froissart has so often been praised for picturesque work, that it is allowable to refine a little about the excellence of this, and to observe that it is plainly dramatic, and only picturesque in an incidental way, the imaginative vision of Froissart being wakened to the picturesque things in the scene—as in that other of the madness of the King of France—by his sympathy with the dramatic life in it. The figure of the king would be nothing much without the suspense of the adventure approaching. What Froissart feels most vividly and with most delight is not the charm of the king's majesty nor yet the accompaniment of Chandos's Almain, the minstrels and the song, but the movement of the hour as it passes, and its effect on the king's mind. The gesture of the king, as his eyes shift to the look-out on the maintop, is what really makes the value of Froissart's description, and the other points in the story are lively because of this interest in the future event. There is nothing very deep or very far fetched in the art of Froissart, but it is not untrue or irrelevant. It aims at the centre, and is kept to its task and carried through it by an instinctive pleasure in the dramatic motives, though these are little elaborated or analysed.

Thus with all his defects he is one of the chief medieval writers, and his work is the culmination of a great medieval school, the school of adventurous history, which begins in those heroic poems of France, whose old forms were still available in Froissart's time for the epic of Bertrand du Guesclin.[1] That poem, however, was the last of its heroic race, and prose had come to be more generally convenient for historical work, as Froissart found in his youth. It had learned some of its capabilities before Froissart began ; indeed, he added little to the school of historical prose except his wider range and his indefatigable spirit. He had models in his pre-decessors for almost everything he did, and he is inferior to some of them in some things. He cannot have more dignity than Villehardouin, more weight of expression than Jean le Bel ; Joinville had more intimate knowledge of the life he wrote about, and his reminiscences come from a deeper source. Froissart completes the older school, however, in a way that was scarce possible later. He carried on the medieval love of adventure and the old simple

[1] *La Vie du vaillant Bertran du Guesclin* (par Cuvelier), edited in *Documents inédits sur l'histoire de France*, 1839 ; a *chanson de geste* in Alexandrines :—

"Seigneurs or escoutez, pour Dieu le roi divin."

methods of story-telling into a time when other
fashions were making themselves evident and claim-
ing to be recognised.   Before the new generations
break in, before the ideals of Petrarch come
into possession of the world, Froissart takes
leisure to look about him, and spends fifty years
in a large comprehensive history, where the life
of the world is represented according to the medieval
traditions of good narrative.   He was well equipped
and well protected.   He had no suspicion nor misgiving about the new fashions, and took no notice of
their allurements; the Humanities and their new
scholarship found him impenitent and insensible.
His humanism was of an older and more Gothic
kind, which very naturally was disparaged as too
quaint and barbarous when the Italian classical rules
of poetry and rhetoric began to dominate the literature of Europe.   But his work remains with that of
the other old French historians to prove how well
the Middle Ages understood some essential principles
of narrative, and even of grammar, when that liberal
art is taken liberally.   He does not indeed represent
all the powers and virtues of medieval literature ;
but though other writers may have gone deeper and
higher, none before him had commanded so wide a
field with so little sign of labour and weariness.
"Wise and imaginative," the terms that he is fond
of using in his praise of kings and lords, are not

inapplicable to Froissart, though the wisdom and imagination may be different from those of the greatest masters. He had at any rate the wisdom that he claimed for himself—of taking things as they came ; and his imagination was of the same kind. It saved him from false rhetoric, and Lord Berners in translating him did more for the humanities than when he adapted the examples of the Spanish rhetorical school. Montaigne, who is entitled to speak for the new age, has given his opinion, and will hardly be contradicted when he pronounces Guevara a little overpraised, or when he discovers something akin to his own freedom in the variety of Froissart.

GASTON PARIS

THE recent death of Gaston Paris was felt as a personal loss by many who had never known him ; such was the influence of his character, exerted through the long series of his published works. It is rarely that an author so purely scientific and specialist, so little inclined to court the popular favour, receives such a tribute of regret. The death of a poet or a novelist may touch a number of people all over the world ; but the death of a man of learning, whose work was conducted always with regard for the subject, and never with any unfair device to catch applause, can seldom make the impression which that of Gaston Paris gave to all who laboured in the same fields. A rare candour and simplicity of aim and procedure made Gaston Paris what he was, and won for him his many friends. The beginners, the half-learned, were drawn into his circle and made partners in his industry, by virtue of the perennial youthfulness of his spirit.

With all his knowledge and all his skill in methods

of work, the product of his long experience, he never grew out of humour with his subject.   In freshness of interest, in the keen appetite for learning, he was the equal of the "juniorest sophister."   This was his genius and his charm.   Those who listened or who read had no need to be afraid of any bondage to formulas, any respectable orthodoxy taking the place of freedom.   Their master was ahead of them all, pressing forward and exploring ; stopping to defend his views only when such a defence was forced upon him as part of the day's work.   Gaston Paris was always more ready to discover new things than to dwell upon his former attainments.   Not that he had any want of respect for positions which he thought he had secured ; his work was too solid for that.   Nor did he try to lighten his studies by forgetting what he had once known, and allowing new interests to drive out the old.   But new interest was unfailing, wherever he turned.   His followers were kept busy ; and that was why they followed him.

Gaston Paris, as a child, received from his father the right of entry into the old literature of France, and never lost the simple pleasure in romances and *chansons de geste*, as poems and stories.   In his university days, keeping still to the subjects in which Paulin Paris was at home, he added a more exact training in philology under Diez at Bonn.   But language did not usurp upon the other province ;

in Germany there was not yet the division between literary and linguistic teaching which is now generally observed, perhaps inevitably. Diez himself, the historian of Provençal poetry and author of the *Comparative Grammar of the Romance Languages*, refused to be limited exclusively to one portion of the field ; and the work of Gaston Paris was comprehensive in the same way. Although literary history was always his chief interest, he did not neglect what is called in the narrower sense philology. He was not wholly occupied with the medieval literature of France. Problems of linguistic science engaged him, as the pages of *Romania* show. It may be that division of labour is more and more required for the progress of these studies ; it is not easy for any one scholar to speak with authority on matters so various as were handled by Gaston Paris. But no number of specialists can quite make up for the genius, wide in range and at the same time discriminating, of the old type of great scholars. The acuteness, the finer work, of Bentley or Lachmann cannot well be taken apart from their substantial historical learning. Gaston Paris had the same sort of ideal. Language cannot be understood from words alone ; and the emendation of a phrase in an old French text might require the help of wide and miscellaneous reading, far away from the immediate matter in hand. There are obvious dangers for the pure scholar in the attractions

R

of historical research ; and it is possible for a narrow man to be more active than one who carries a burden of learning.   But the greatest scholars are not "word-catchers, that live on syllables"; they find it possible to be both strong in the weighty matters and alert with the more subtle problems, as Gaston Paris was.

He learned much from his father, as has been said already, and he carried on his work.   Paulin Paris[1] represented an older stage of interest in medieval French—older methods and views, mainly of the eighteenth century, with some colouring from the Romantic school.   His manner often recalls that of Scott in his antiquarian essays, *e.g.* the introduction to *Sir Tristrem*, or, from an earlier generation, that of Warton's *History of English Poetry*.   He writes like a free man, as if it were all for his own pleasure, whatever amount of industry he may have put into his description of *chansons de geste*, or romances of the Round Table, or French lyric poetry of the thirteenth century.   He refused to be pitied for the time spent in "deciphering" old manuscripts.

Car pour moi je ne demande pas qu'on me sache le moindre gré de les avoir déchiffrés. En effet, combien d'heures ai-je vues passer rapidement en poursuivant cette lecture ! Combien de romans du jour et de gazettes ai-je

---

[1] *Notice sur Paulin Paris*, 1881 ; see also *La poésie du moyen âge*, i. p. 211 *et seq.*

fermés pour étudier plus longtemps ces admirables compositions, images de l'esprit, des mœurs et des croyances de nos
ancêtres ! Combien de fois alors n'ai-je pas mis un frein à
mon enthousiasme, en me rappelant avec une sorte d'effroi
l'aventure du chevalier de la Manche ! Honnête Don
Quichotte ! les romans coupables de ta folie n'étaient que
de longues paraphrases décolorées des *Chansons de Geste* ; que
serais-tu devenu si tu avais lu les originaux ![1]

Yet, deeply plunged as he was in the literature of
the Middle Ages, full of knowledge and enjoyment
of all the things that appealed to the Romantic school,
Paulin Paris at the same time judged his ground with
a rational and sceptical coolness, and never forced
his admiration or allowed it to interfere with his
historical sense. His controversy with Fauriel, over
the hypothesis of a Provençal origin for French epic,
is still delightful reading for the ease with which
he manages the discussion and corrects the too
enthusiastic reasoning of the other side. Gaston
Paris, with a much severer training, followed the
same tradition, and displayed, though in a different
way, the same enjoyment of medieval literature, the
same good sense in criticism.

Neither Paulin Paris nor his son belonged to the
Romantic school, though they passed their time
among the books and in the centuries from which
modern romantic poets are supposed to have drawn

---

[1] Preface to *Garin le Loherain* (1833), p. iii. ; quoted by Gaston Paris
in his account of his father, *op. cit.* p. 217.

their most effective scenery, properties, ideals, and emotions.   Paulin Paris was glad to call the attention of poets to the riches of the *chansons de geste*, but it did not matter to him very much whether they took his advice or not.   He had his books, and could use them for his own profit or entertainment whatever the contemporary fashion might be.   In spite of the humorous reference to Don Quixote, his very sincere delight in the old heroic poems was never wrought up to the extreme romantic pitch. Like George Ellis, and like Scott himself, he kept a sane estimate of medieval romance.   Gaston Paris was equally free from any extravagant romanticism, but not quite in the same manner.   It was not the old-fashioned ironical worldliness of the eighteenth century that determined his views and tastes.   The second half of the nineteenth century never escaped from the romantic influence, however it might protest and rebel ; the realists are all romanticists disguised —" unfrocked," as Flaubert expressed it.   Men of learning were of course protected from the violent revolutions that tormented the poets and novelists ; some were drawn to the Middle Ages by purely scientific motives, with a positive prejudice to begin with against all the " Gothic " fascinations of the romantic tradition.[1]   But Gaston Paris was not one

[1] Cf. *La poésie du moyen âge*, i. p. 213, for the "conversion" of Victor Le Clerc.

of these ; he had learned from the Romantic school
all that it had to teach regarding the Middle Ages
and the interpretation of their art ; he had gone
further on ways of his own, but in his sober judgment of values, even when pointing out the faults,
the flatness, the puerilities of medieval literature, he
always kept a sense of the old charm, of the magic
still recoverable in *Tristan* and in many less famous
stories.

The French Romantic school was not so deep in
learning as the schools of some other countries :
there was no poet who, like Scott or Uhland, worked
hard in antiquarian prose to collect and edit and
explain the poetry of the Middle Ages. Victor
Hugo's romantic ornament is borrowed from all
lands and tongues : a tribute levied on mild historians
without respect for their feelings—

> Écoutez tous, marquis venus de la montagne,
> Duc Gerhard, Sire Uther, pendragon de Bretagne,
> Burgrave Darius, burgrave Cadwalla !

Among the lighter essays of Gaston Paris is one
(appended to *Les sept infants de Lara* in *Poèmes
et légendes*) that traces in an amusing way one of
the medieval inspirations of Victor Hugo : in M.
Demaison's introduction to *Aimeri de Narbonne*
may be found the sources of the poet's *Aymerillot*,
showing the same masterful ease and unconcern in
turning the most casual knowledge to good account

in immortal verse. By which it is not proved, nor intended, that *Aymerillot* is less poetical than it seems to be ; only that Victor Hugo was not a student of the same sort as Scott or Uhland. The Romantic school in France, so far as it dealt with the Middle Ages, was dependent upon the men of learning, and not to any great extent a sharer in their historical work.

Gaston Paris, coming after the romantic days, carried on the researches that had preceded them. How continuous the labour has been, and how enormous, may be partly realised in looking at the thirty-two volumes of the *Histoire littéraire de la France*, begun by the Benedictines in 1733, and now brought down, " vaster than empires and more slow," as far as the fourteenth century. In that great work the ideas of 1830 may be found here and there reflected, but they are only an accident, a passing radiance : the substantial life is hardly touched by them.

The study of Old French as it is understood by Gaston Paris and his associates and pupils is the same kind of work as the study of antiquity, Greek or Latin, carried on at the time of the revival of learning. They have the same trust in the value of the subject, the same sort of ambition and appetite for universal knowledge, including in its scope everything ascertainable in political or social history,

every document of the time, with the most effective
instruments of criticism to explain them. Their
business is historical, in the original liberal meaning
of the term history. The spirit of curiosity about
the past is their chief motive ; no appliance or
apparatus is neglected that can add to the store of
knowledge.

In an essay on Gaston Paris written some years
ago,[1] M. Jules Lemaître described the processes of
medieval research in terms that might have held
good of Browning's Grammarian. Historical learning, he says (and the text of his sermon is the work
of Gaston Paris), has no thought of any immediate
use for its discoveries ; labour is bestowed on minute
things, in the faith that some day they may be turned
to account. The history of the Middle Ages grows
like a coral island, by the aggregated lives of many
workers. This is not the whole truth. Few indeed
of the contributors to the *Histoire littéraire* have
allowed the pursuit of knowledge to be hindered or
diverted by doubts or scruples about the immediate
value of each step. It is in this that the modern
scholar, the successor of the Benedictines in their
industry, differs from the dilettante of the Romantic
school. Many things are included in the *Histoire
littéraire* and in *Romania* that are of no obvious use
to the literary artist. It is not on every page that a

[1] *Les Contemporains*, troisième série, p. 219.

suggestion like that of *Aymerillot* may be found; and a discussion of the terminations in *-ain* has little connection—much less than "*hoti's* business"—with the inspiration or the interpretation of poetry.

But Gaston Paris thought of more than the accumulation of facts or the working out of historical and philological details. He was a humanist; and his labours were directed by the same ideal as those of the founders of classical learning. He studied the history of old French literature, not by way of opposition to the humanities of Greece and Rome, but as an extension of the same domain. He had a full sense of all the respects in which *Roland* comes short of the *Iliad*, in which the fluent simplicity of old French verse is inferior to the Greek art of poetry; yet he believed that the French epics have things to tell worth listening to, and that there is a lesson of style, not only of mythology, in the intricate romances of Arthur.[1]

His genius as a critic of literature equalled his industry as historian and philologist. Of all his achievements, if not the greatest, at any rate that of which it is easiest to speak outside of the school, is that, in a long series of writings, with every variety of scale and immediate purpose, he has explained the

---

[1] See for example the comparison of the Anglo-Norman Thomas, the chief authority for the story of Tristan, with his more refined contemporary Chrétien de Troyes (*Poèmes et légendes*).

growth of old French poetry and prose in all their
kinds, and has judged their present literary value
as securely as he worked out technical points of
history or scholarship. It is not everything, but it
is the aspect of his work most convenient for this
place, that he was one of the great critics of French
literature. His preface to the *History of French
Literature*, edited by Petit de Julleville, is a summary
of the whole matter, down to the Renaissance and
beyond, written with an insight into general causes
such as is often desired but seldom attained in the
work of other critics. In the certainty with which
the lines are drawn it resembles St. Evremond's
comparison and interpretation of the French and
English genius, probably the most successful piece
of generalisation ever made by any writer on such
subjects ; while the general view is enlivened with
exact knowledge of details. This essay explains
the peculiar character of the French Renaissance,
the reason of the wide difference between the
Middle Ages and the sixteenth century in France,
bringing out the peculiar character of the fifteenth
century—

une littérature bâtarde, sorte de Renaissance avortée, mêlant
les restes de la puérilité subtile du moyen âge à une gauche
imitation de l'antiquité latine. (Preface, p. 9)—

a kind of waste interval—empty, pretentious—at the

back of which lay the right medieval poetry, un-
known to Ronsard and his companions. Then
follows the description of this older literature, in
terms that prove its affinity with all that is most
characteristic of the French nation in modern times,
its talent for clear language, a perfect sympathy and
understanding between the author and his audience.
From this virtue of lucidity comes also (as St. Evremond has remarked in comparing French and English) a certain shallowness : the personages in French
epic or French drama are not fully realised ; more or
less they are abstract, they represent ideas.

On chercherait en vain dans toute l'Europe médiévale une
œuvre qui incarne comme la *Chanson de Roland* les façons
de sentir, sinon de la nation tout entière, au moins de la
partie active et dominante de la nation, dans ce qu'elles
eurent de plus impersonnel et de plus élevé. De là cette
faiblesse de la caractéristique qu'on a relevée dans notre
vieille épopée : les individus l'intéressent moins que les idées
et les sentiments dont ils sont les porteurs. (*Ib.*)

A similar quality is proved to exist in the other
kinds of old poetry, in the courtly romances of
the twelfth century, in the fabliaux ; Lancelot and
Renard, the hero and the picaroon, are both of them,
in Old French, rather abstract types.

Leurs traits sont d'autant plus significatifs qu'ils sont moins
personnels, et se gravent d'autant mieux dans le souvenir
qu'ils sont coordonnés par une logique parfaite. Ils gagnent

en relief et en clarté tout ce qu'ils perdent en profondeur et
en complication. N'est-ce pas aussi ce qu'on peut dire des créa-
tions les plus parfaites de notre littérature classique ? (*Ib.*)

Then Gaston Paris brings out the peculiar excellence of the romantic poetry of France in the
twelfth and thirteenth centuries, so seldom understood
beyond the borders by the Teutonic nations who
imported French novels and adapted them.

La tendance à créer des types, plutôt qu'à essayer de faire
vivre des individus dans toute leur complexité changeante,
n'exclut pas l'analyse psychologique ; au contraire. Les
sentiments humains sont étudiés en eux-mêmes, dans leur
évolution logique et leurs conflits, tels que, dans des conditions données, ils doivent se produire, chez tout homme
défini d'une certaine façon ; et ceux qui les éprouvent
aiment à se les expliquer à eux-mêmes . . . pour l'instruction des autres. Cette analyse psychologique, la littérature
française y a excellé dans tous les temps. On pourrait
citer tel morceau de Chrétien de Troyes qui ne le cède
pas en vérité, en ingéniosité, parfois en subtilité, aux plus
célèbres monologues de nos tragédies, aux pages les plus
fouillées de nos romans contemporains. (*Ib.*)

Following which comes a note on the *Romance of the
Rose*, *l'épopée psychologique*, as it were the ghost or
shadow of all the sentiment in the school of Chrétien
de Troyes, disembodied "states of mind" moving
about as persons in a story. The discussion of
French medieval style, after this, is equally sure of
its ground, and in the same way impartial ; setting
down all the common faults, platitude, triviality,

but not concealing the delight with which the critic turns to the ancient writers, nor ignoring the true beauty of their work.

Mais leur langue n'est pas seulement claire : elle a souvent une justesse, une légèreté, une aisance naturelle qui font penser aux meilleurs morceaux de notre littérature des deux derniers siècles. Ils voient bien et savent dire avec netteté ce qu'ils ont vu ; leur parole les amuse et nous amuse avec eux. Beaucoup d'entre eux sont d'aimables causeurs, un peu babillards, qui se laissent d'autant plus volontiers aller à leur verve qu'ils voient que leurs auditeurs y prennent plaisir ; d'autres sont d'excellents raisonneurs, qui cherchent sérieusement à convaincre ou à intéresser leur public, et qui y réussissent par la simplicité et la précision de leur exposition ; d'autres encore ont su imprimer à leurs discours de la grandeur, de la sensibilité ou de la finesse. (*Ib.*)

Gaston Paris himself, in his writing, had that instinctive clearness which he finds constant in French literature—that same regard for his hearers which, in the earliest authors of his nation, as he points out, distinguished the even, plain discourse of the *chansons de geste* from the more high-flown heroic poetry of other nations. At the same time his literary judgment, moving so freely among generalisations, was always based on particulars—a different thing from the peremptory opinions of less patient critics. Popular literary history, working at some distance from its subject, may pronounce that one *chanson de geste* is just like any other *chanson de geste*. Gaston Paris, with complete appreciation of all the habitual ways, the

repetitions, the want of care, the ready use of common forms and stop-gaps (*décourageantes chevilles*),
in Old French epic, knew well also that under superficial uniformity there were differences of genius and
temper clearly marked ; and that to confound Balzac
and Stendhal, or Corneille and Racine, on account of
their common qualities would be hardly a stronger
proof of critical incompetence than (for example) a
refusal to distinguish the merits of *Roland* and *Raoul
de Cambrai*. He treated old French poetry with
the same conscience and the same discernment as
the greatest critics have given to the greatest masters.
He did not exaggerate the value of his authors ;
but the fact that they did not belong to the seventeenth or the nineteenth century was for him no
reason to treat them under different rules or with less
precision.

Perhaps the essays in which he showed his learning and his critical power to best advantage are those
on the Arthurian romances, in *Romania* and the
Histoire littéraire (tome xxx.). He had to discover
their sources and trace their development—a business
sometimes pursued without much regard for qualities
of literature. Gaston Paris, studying the transmission
of popular tales from obscure Celtic origins to the
schools of French poetry in the twelfth century, did
not keep to what is called folklore, though this was a
large part of his work. It was not enough for him

to trace the progress of a fable through different stages, or merely to verify the fact that similar plots, incidents, characters, or names were found in different versions, in different languages.   Along with this he watched the literary motives of the poets, the influences of fashion or of individual temper that made them change and remould the folklore substance.

An example of his procedure may be found in the description of *Guinglain*, a poem of Renaud de Beaujeu, in which the simple fairy-tale of "Li beaux Desconus" is incongruously decorated to indulge the rhetorical and sentimental taste of an ambitious literary man.   Problems much more complex are solved in the essay on *Le Chevalier de la Charrette*, *i.e.* the *Lancelot* of Chrétien de Troyes (*Romania*, vol. x. p. 459 *et seq.*).   Peculiar insight and judgment were required to distinguish the shadows in this illusory realm : the result, which proves the dependence of Lancelot on the doctrine of the troubadours, and establishes the relation between the narrative poetry of France and the lyric of Provence, is gained by a masterly use of every available instrument.   Historical study of the facts (*e.g.* of the part taken by Marie de Champagne in bringing Provençal ideas to the north) is completed and enlightened by critical intuition and sympathy.

Another talent is displayed in the short history of medieval French literature.   This is a book for the

schools, compact and positive, with little room either
for eloquence or for historical detail. Yet, along
with its serried names and dates, it presents, at the
smallest cost of words, a critical estimate of every
matter it touches. On a larger scale the *Villon*, one
of the author's latest works, is perhaps the finest
example of his powers. In the description of Villon's
poetry, and more especially, perhaps, in the account
of his poetical education, there is the fruit of a whole
lifetime of research and reflection. Villon and his
age are shown in their relation to the poetry of the
preceding centuries : the decline of the earlier literature, the strange obliteration of the older poetry,
the rise and decay of new schools in the fourteenth
century, the vacancy and vanity of the fifteenth, are
all brought out, in the author's inimitably simple
manner, as a setting for the new genius of Villon.
Often and well as Villon has been praised, this mode
of approaching his work was needed ; and no one
else could have used it to the same effect, with so sure
a control of all the history.

Many of the friends of Gaston Paris have written
lately about his personal influence. Such regret as
they feel was felt and expressed by Gaston Paris himself in the memorial notices that he wrote on James
Darmesteter and Renan—passages of meditation, full
of dignity, not effusive, which perhaps convey as
much as a stranger need seek to know about his

more intimate thoughts.   It may not be out of place
to mention here the generous phrase in his *Villon*,
returning thanks for the liberal gift of his friend
Marcel Schwob, who, surrendering the interests of
his own book, made over the results of his independent researches to be used in the biography.   And
further, there is one aspect of the private life of
Gaston Paris which it is well to remember—the grace
and rectitude of his dealing with scholars outside of
France.   He believed strongly in his own country,
and hardly less strongly in the community of learning over all the world.   Two papers of his, composed
during the Franco-Prussian war, illustrate the two
loyalties, which he was able to reconcile without
diluting either of them.   One is the lecture on
" Roland," in December 1870, repeating the old
prayer—

> Ne placet Deu ne ses saintismes angles
> Que ja par mei perdet sa valor France !

The other is one of his more technical pieces (on
a Latin poem about Frederick Barbarossa), written
during the siege of Paris.[1]   It mentions calmly his
regret that he is prevented from consulting German

---

[1] The war interrupted the work of a young German scholar in Paris,
Julius Brakelmann, who had to leave half printed the *Corpus* of Old
French lyric poetry which he was editing.   He was killed, fighting
against the French, at Mars la Tour, in July 1870 ; the fragment of
his book was published in 1891 as he had left it, with a note simply
stating the facts, more impressive than any rhetoric.

scholars : " They are separated from us by their armies and our ramparts, or engaged perhaps in the preparations for an attack upon our city." Gaston Paris knew to the full the claims of patriotism and of learning, and tampered with neither when they were accidentally opposed.

In England he had many personal friends, besides many more who were indebted to him through his writings—attracted almost unconsciously by the character as well as the matter of his work. There was no display, no emphasis in his style. But everything he wrote gave the impression of efficiency and sincerity, or rather of an intellectual magnanimity in which all the other excellences are included.

INDEX

259

Printed by R. & R. CLARK, LIMITED, *Edinburgh*.

WORKS ON THE
HISTORY AND CRITICISM OF LITERATURE

History of English Poetry. By WILLIAM JOHN COURTHOPE, C.B., M.A. Vol. I.—The Middle Ages—The Influence of the Roman Empire—The Encyclopædic Education of the Church—The Feudal System. Vol. II.—The Renaissance and the Reformation : Influence of the Court and the Universities. Vol. III.—The Intellectual Conflict of the Seventeenth Century — Decadent Influence of the Feudal Monarchy — Growth of the National Genius. Vol. IV.—Development and Decline of the Poetical Drama—Influence of the Court and the People. 8vo. 10s. net each volume. [*Vol. V. in the Press.*]

Life in Poetry : Law in Taste. Two Series of Lcetures delivered in Oxford, 1895-1900. By W. J. COURTHOPE, C.B. 8vo. 10s. net.

A History of Early English Literature. By Rev. STOPFORD A. BROOKE. Two Vols. 8vo. 20s. net.

Romances of Roguery : An Episode in the History of the Novel. By FRANK WADLEIGH CHANDLER. In two parts. Part I.—The Picaresque Novel in Spain. Globe 8vo. 8s. 6d. net.

The English Heroic Play. By LEWIS N. CHASE. Globe 8vo. 8s. 6d. net.

Studies in German Literature in the Nineteenth Century. By J. F. COAR. 8vo. 10s. 6d. net.

Abridged History of Greek Literature. By MM. ALFRED and MAURICE CROISET. Translated by G. F. HEFFELBOWER. 8vo. 10s. 6d. net.

The Development of the English Novel. By W. L. CROSS. Globe 8vo. 6s.

Frédéric Mistral, Poet and Leader in Provence. By Prof. C. A. DOWNER. Globe 8vo. 6s. net.

The Italian Renaissance in England. By L. EINSTEIN. Globe 8vo. 6s. net.

The Elizabethan Lyric. By JOHN ERSKINE, Ph.D. Globe 8vo. 6s. 6d. net.

The Beginnings of Poetry. By Prof. F. B. GUMMERE. 8vo. 12s. 6d. net.

MACMILLAN AND CO., LIMITED, LONDON

WORKS ON THE HISTORY AND CRITICISM OF LITERATURE—
continued.

The Masters of English Literature. By STEPHEN GWYNN. Globe 8vo. 3s. 6d.

The Indebtedness of Chaucer's "Troilus and Criseyde" to Guido Delle Colonne's "Historia Trojana." By GEORGE L. HAMILTON, A.M. Crown 8vo. 5s. net.

Platonism in English Poetry of the 16th and 17th Centuries. By J. S. HARRISON. Globe 8vo. 8s. 6d. net.

History of English Literature.—In Four Volumes. Crown 8vo.

> **English Literature from the Beginning to the Norman Conquest.** By STOPFORD A. BROOKE, M.A. 7s. 6d.
>
> **Elizabethan Literature (1560-1665).** By GEORGE SAINTSBURY. 7s. 6d.
>
> **Eighteenth Century Literature (1660-1780).** By EDMUND GOSSE, M.A. 7s. 6d.
>
> **Nineteenth Century Literature (1780-1900).** By G. SAINTSBURY. 7s. 6d.

Renascence of the English Drama. By HENRY ARTHUR JONES. Crown 8vo. 6s.

Studies in Montaigne. Early Writing of Montaigne. By GRACE NORTON. Two Vols. Globe 8vo. 12s. 6d. net.

A Short History of English Literature. By Prof. GEORGE SAINTSBURY. Crown 8vo. 8s. 6d.

English Chronicle Play. By FELIX E. SCHELLING. Crown 8vo. 8s. 6d. net.

A History of Literary Criticism in the Renaissance. With Special Reference to Influence of Italy in the Formation and Development of Modern Classicism. By J. E. SPINGARN. Crown 8vo. 6s. net.

The Evolution of the English Novel. By F. H. STODDARD. Globe 8vo. 6s.

The Classical Heritage of the Middle Ages. By H. O. TAYLOR. Globe 8vo. 7s. 6d. net.

The Language and Metre of Chaucer. By BERNHARD TEN BRINK. Revised by F. KLUGE. Translated by M. BENTINCK SMITH. Crown 8vo. 6s. net.

Spanish Literature in the England of the Tudors. By J. G. UNDERHILL. Crown 8vo. 8s. 6d. net.

A History of English Dramatic Literature, to the Death of Queen Anne. By ADOLPHUS WILLIAM WARD, Litt.D. Second Edition. Three Vols. 8vo. 36s. net.

MACMILLAN AND CO., LIMITED, LONDON